I0481731

Emoji Funny Face : Coloring book

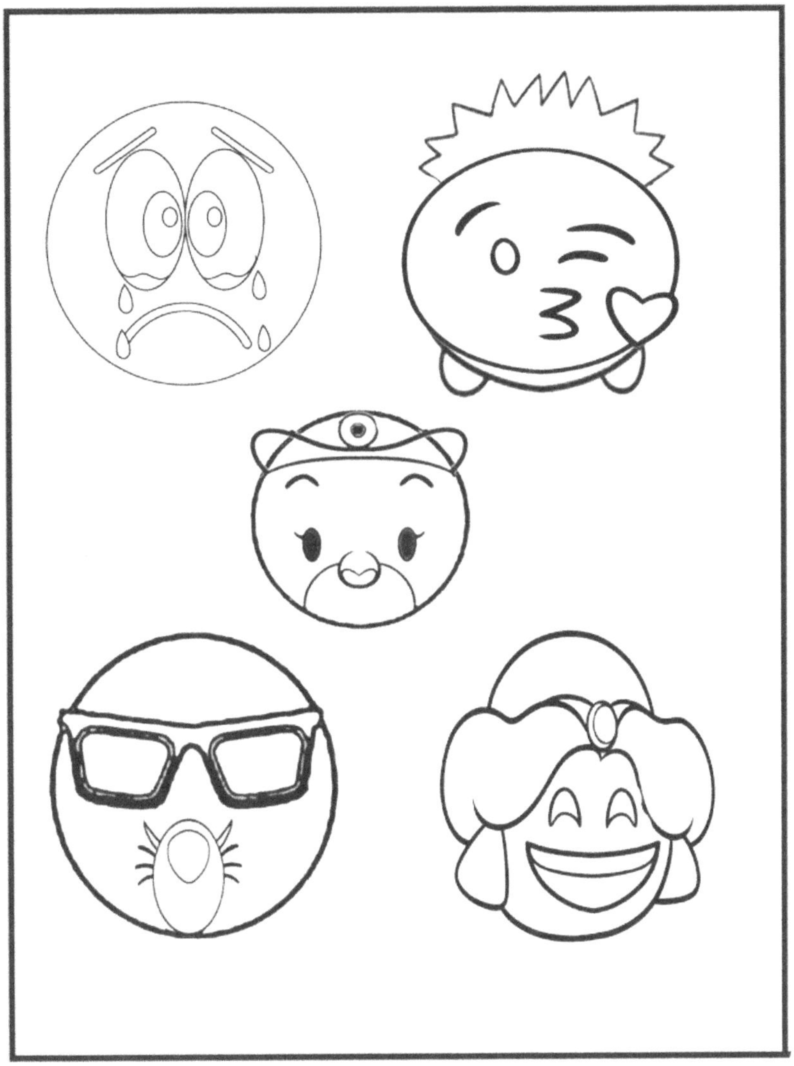

Nina Packer

Emoji Funny Face Coloring Activity Book

ISBN-13: 978-1983538858

ISBN-10: 198353885X

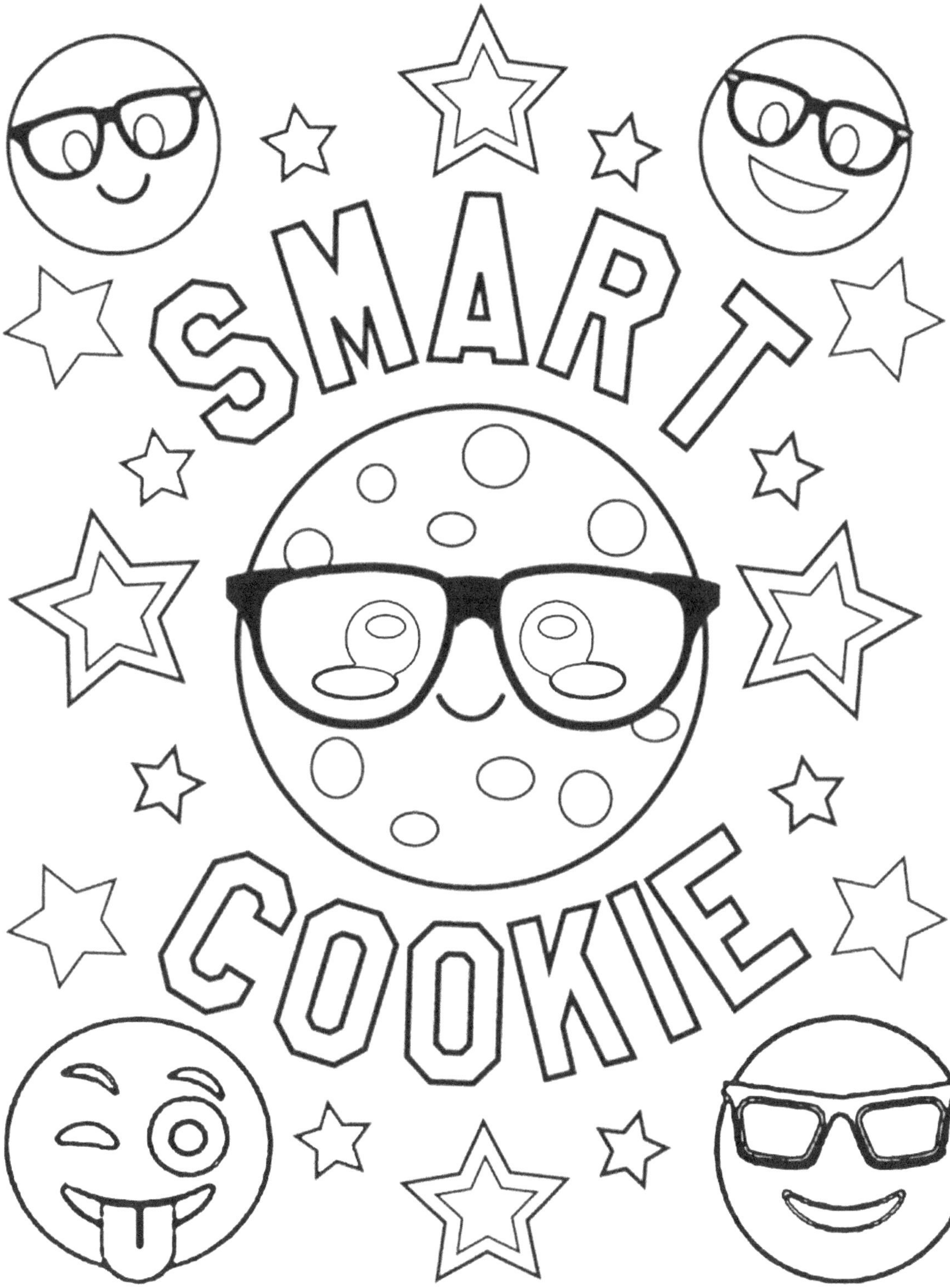
SMART
COOKIE

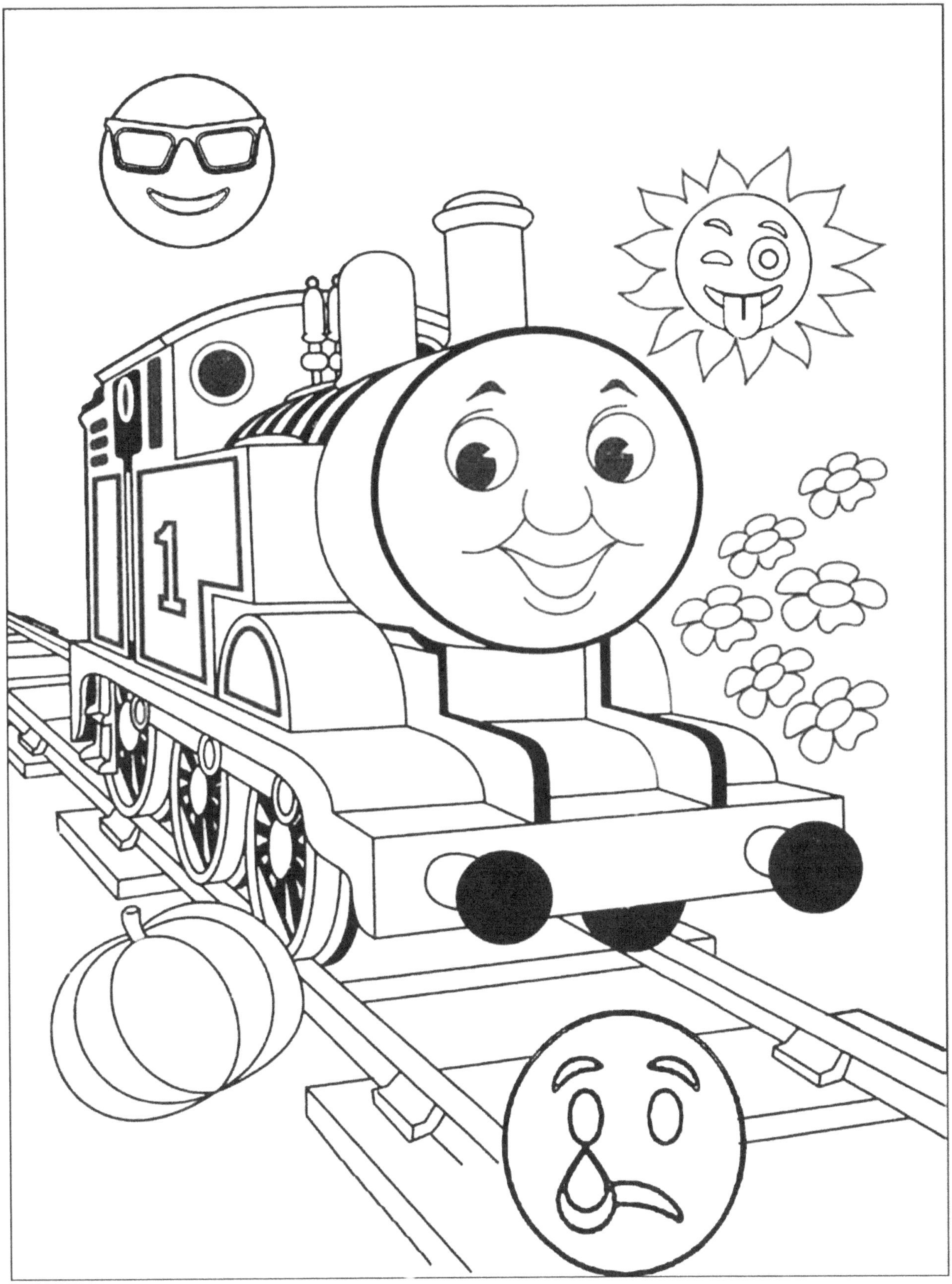

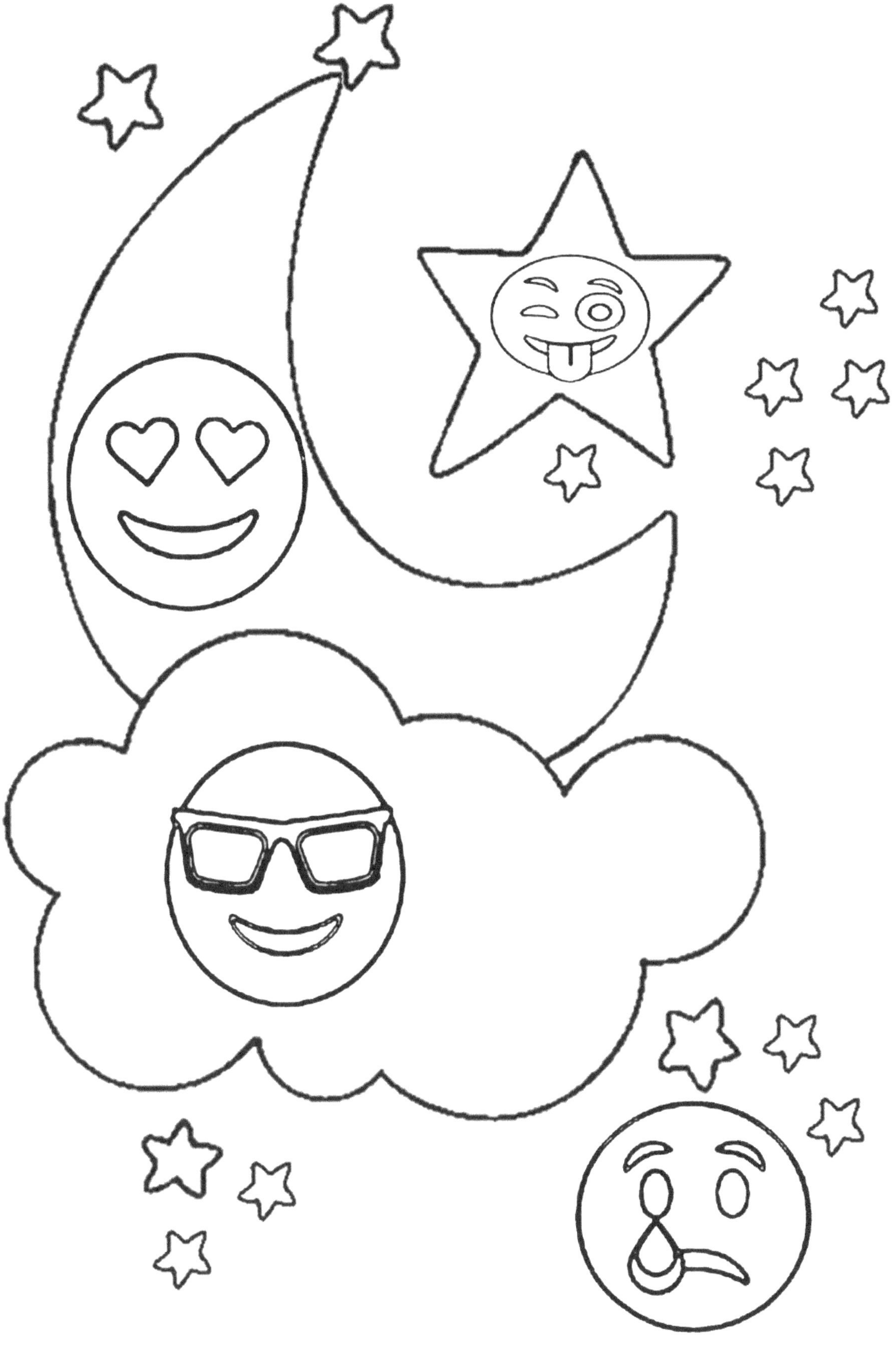

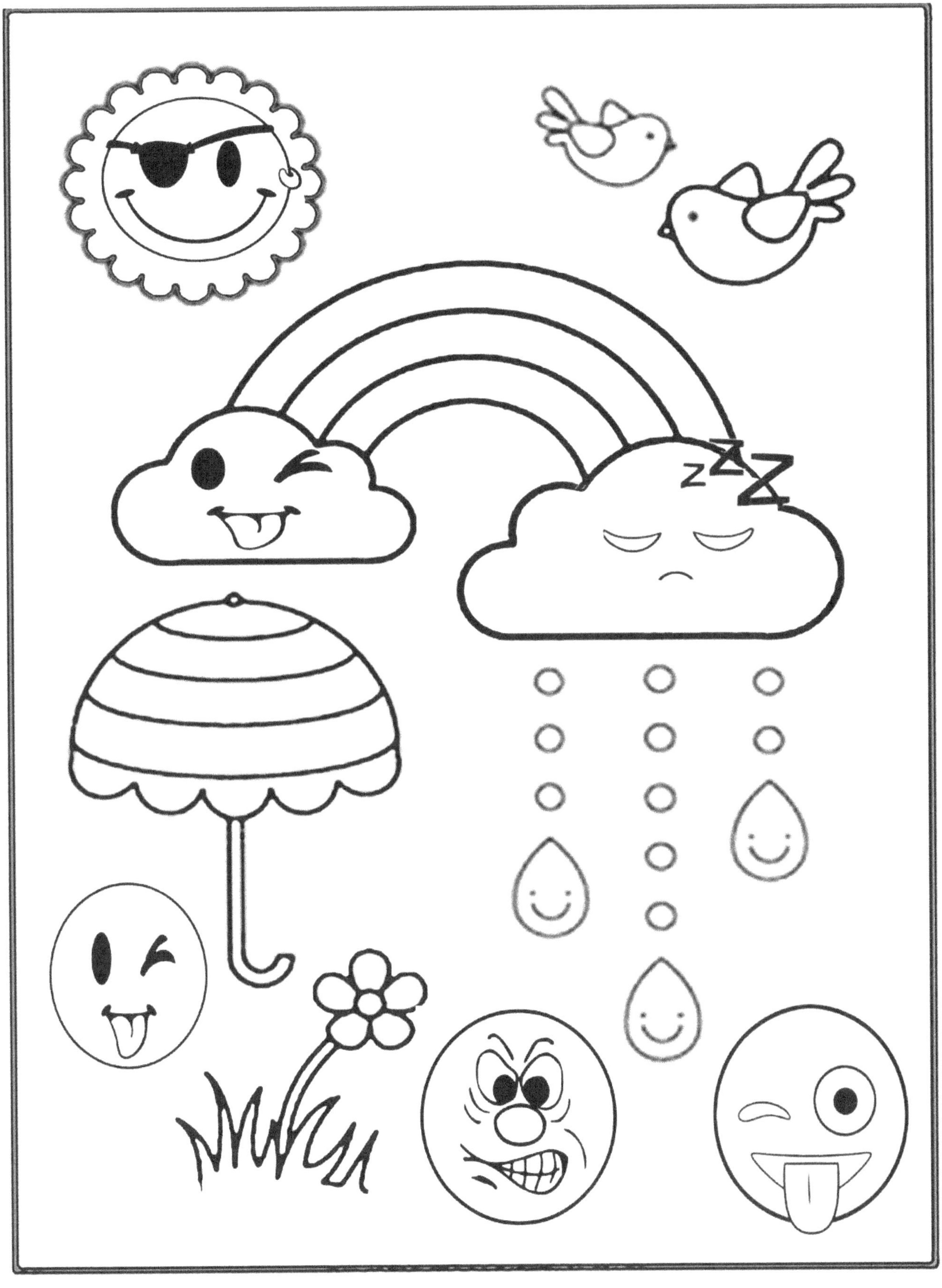
zZZ

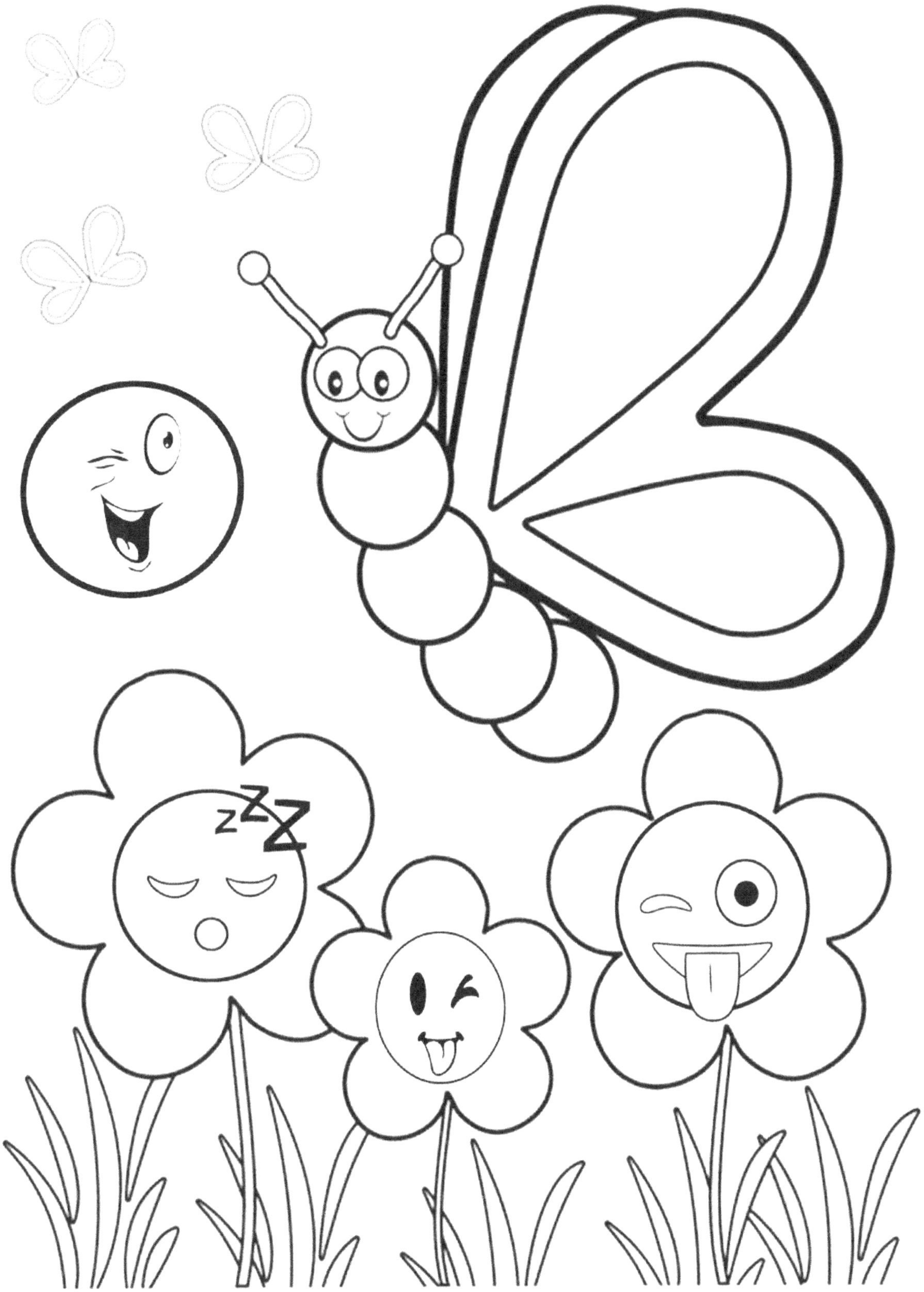

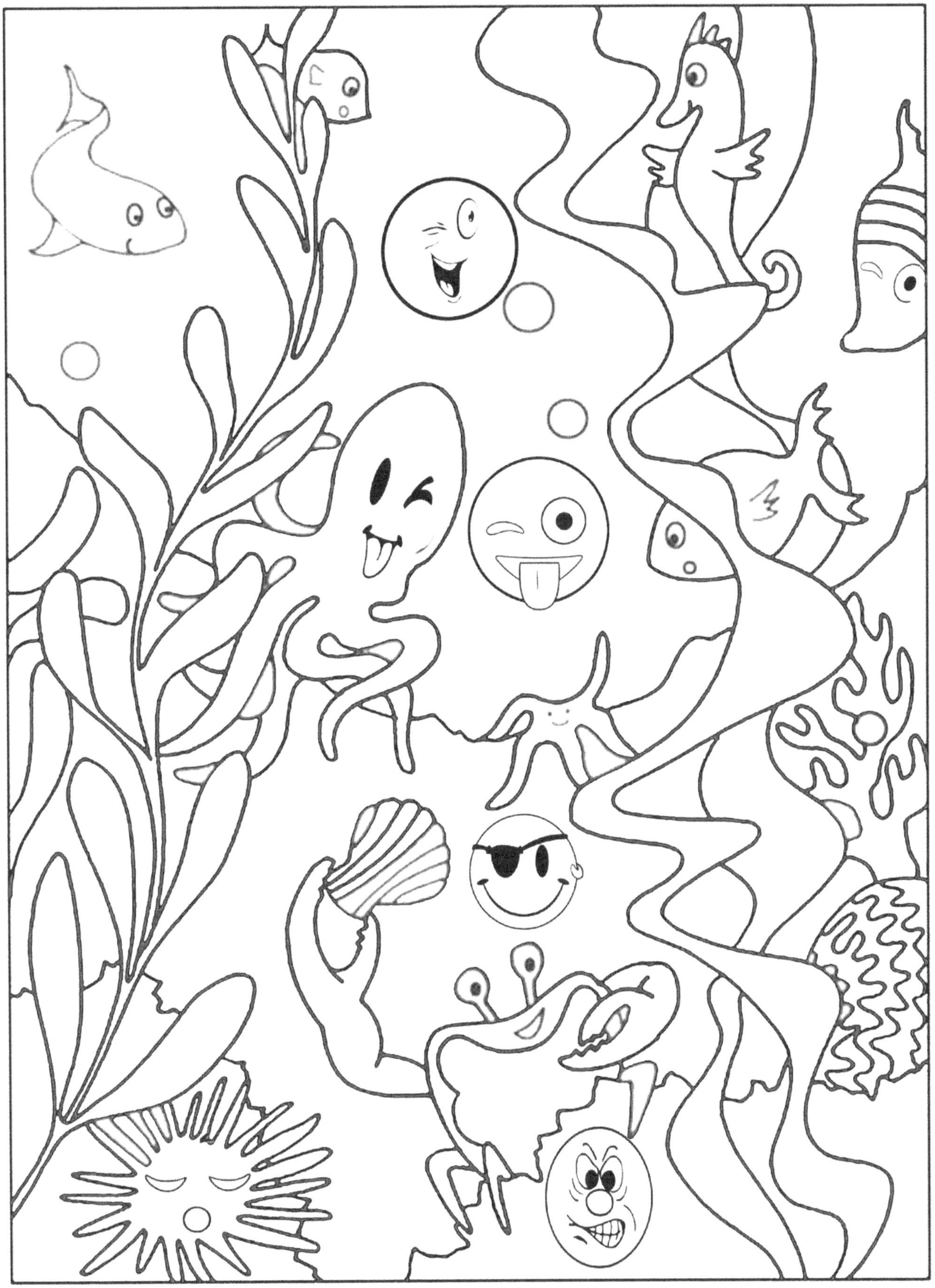

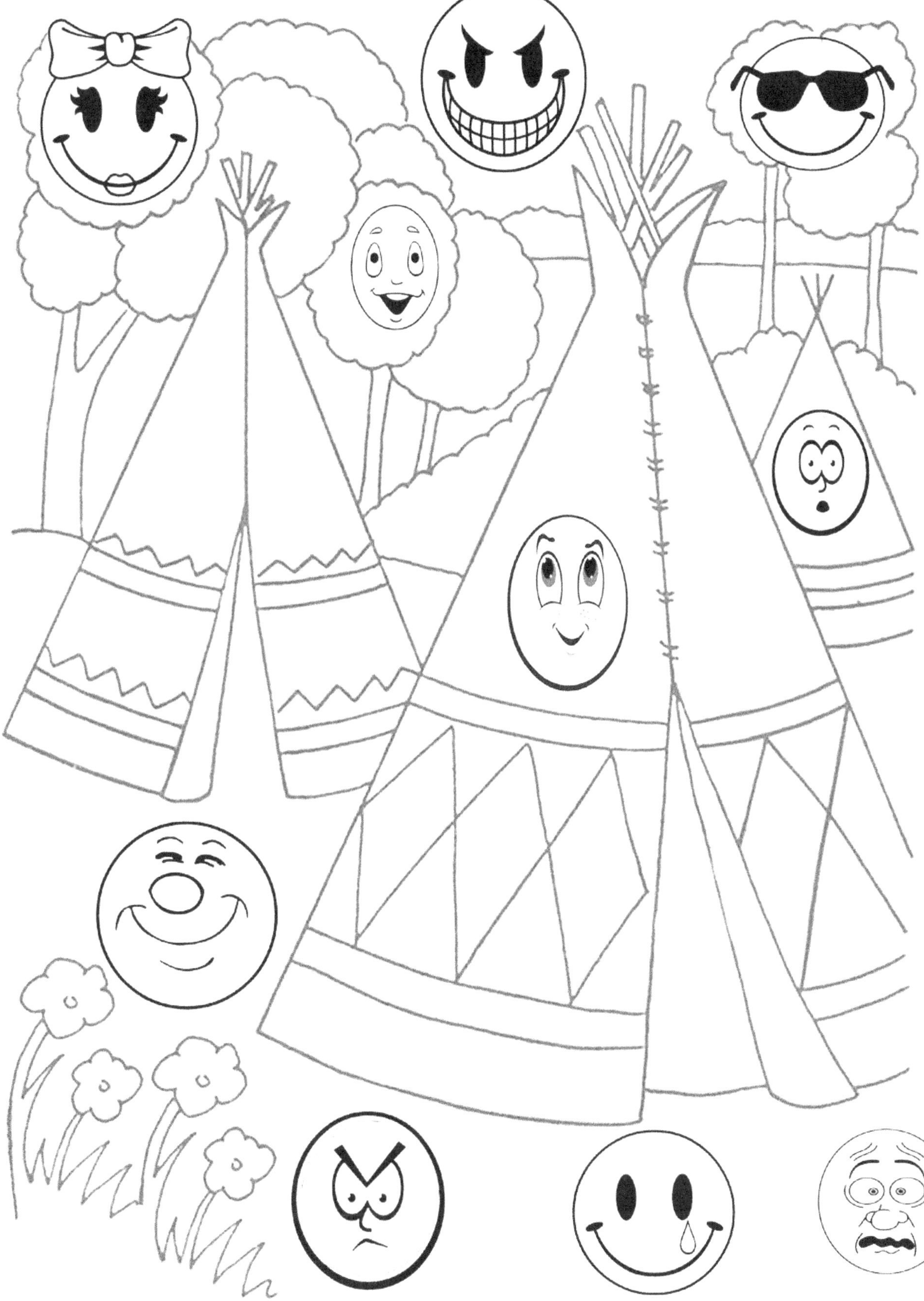

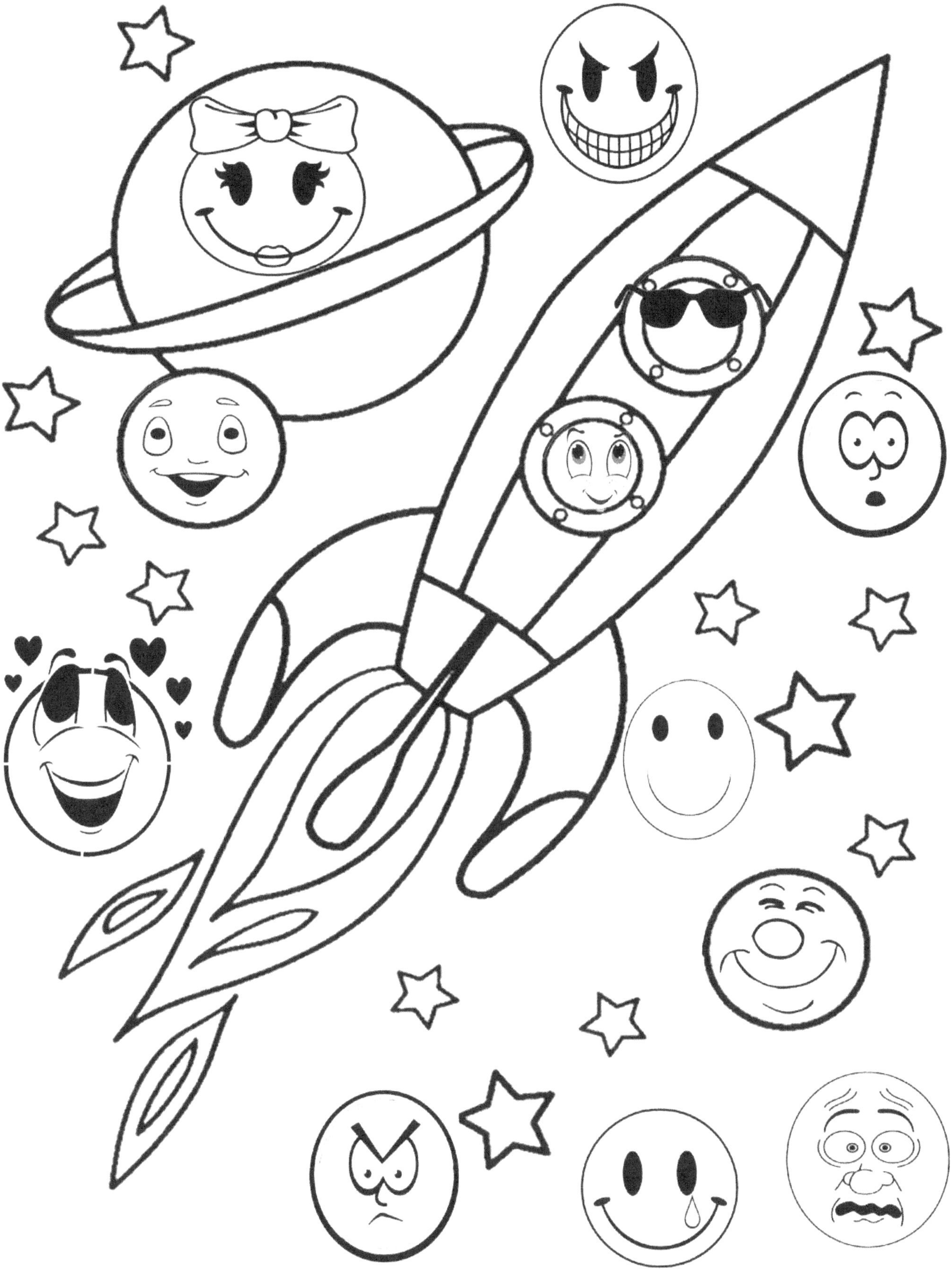

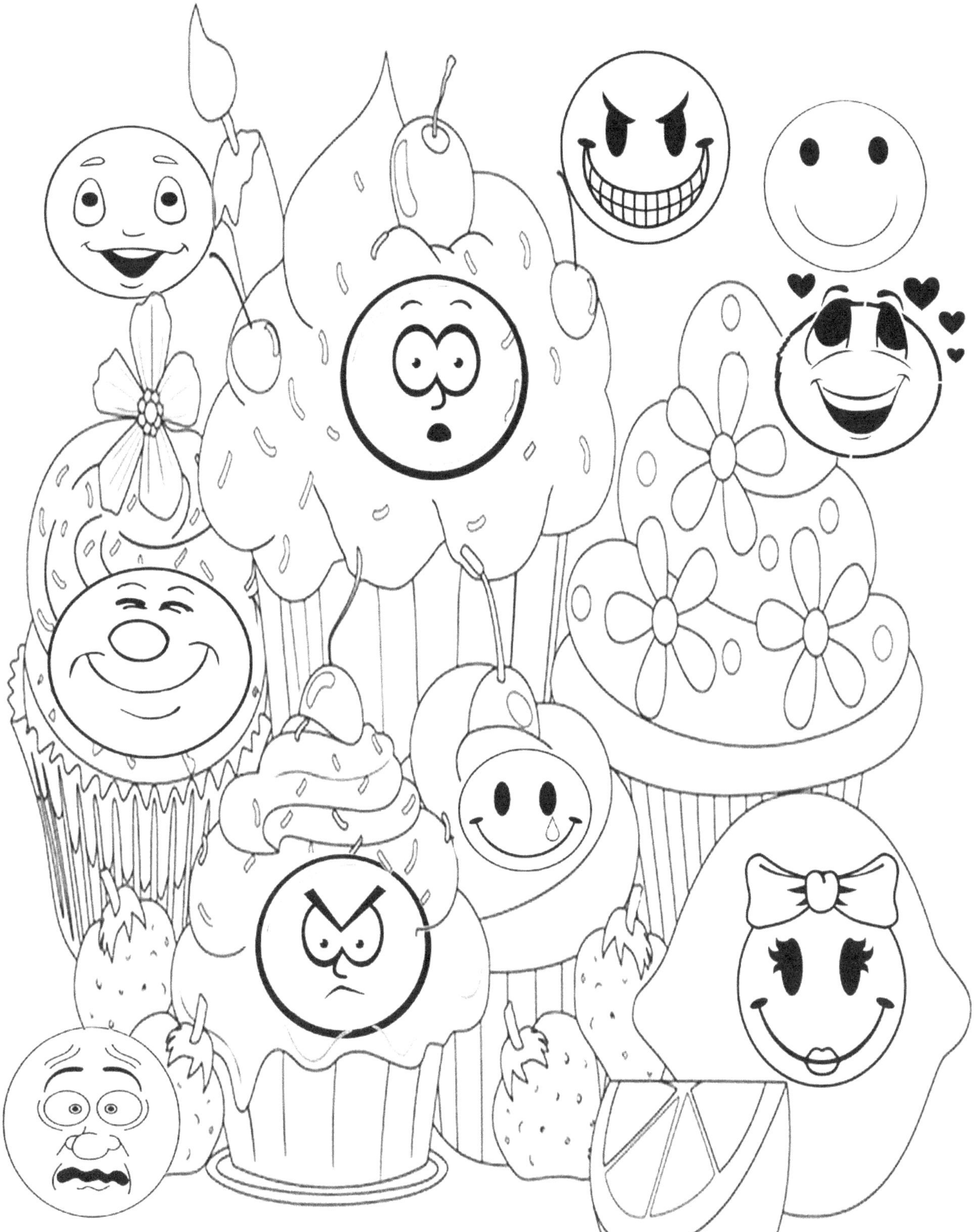

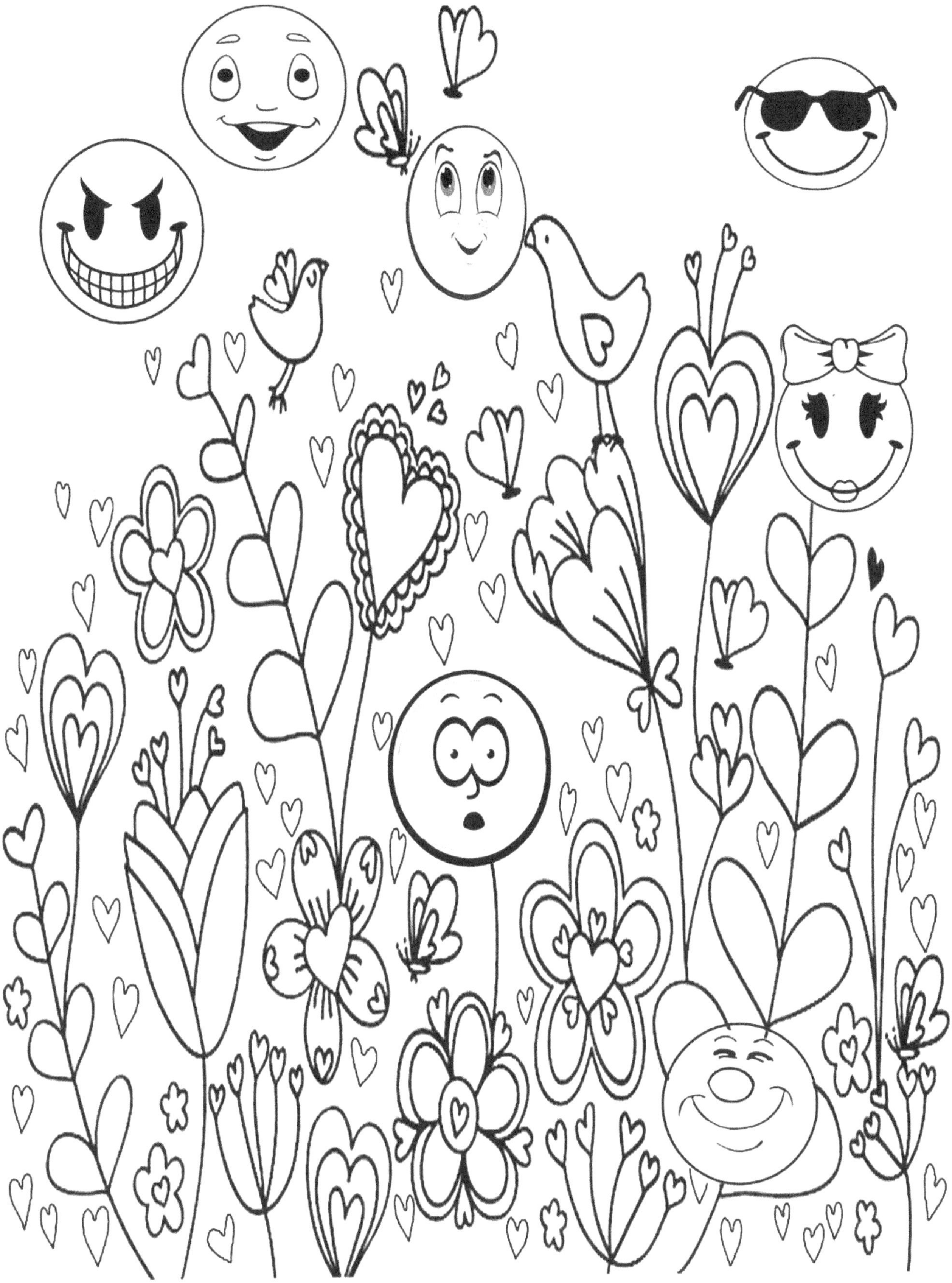

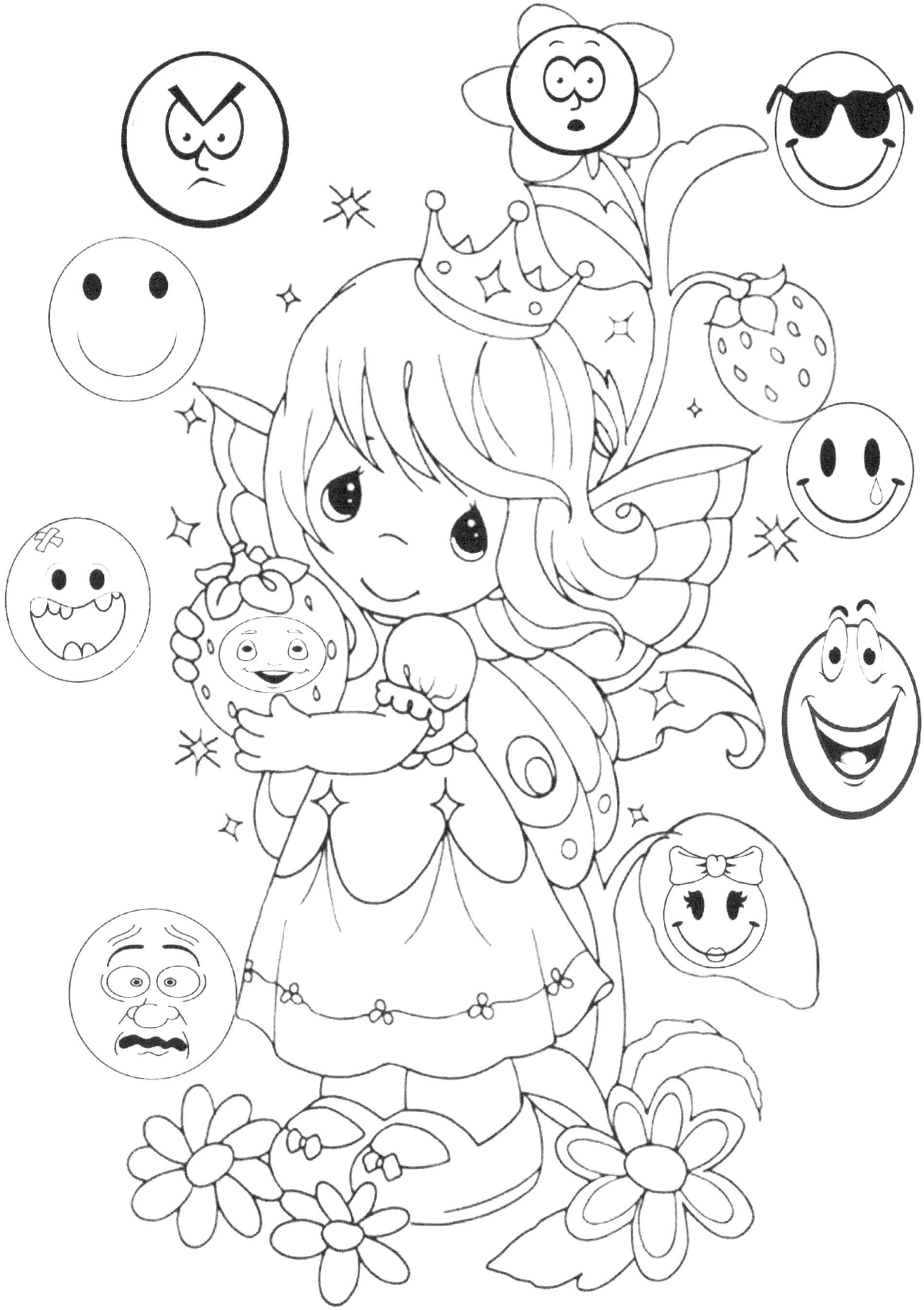

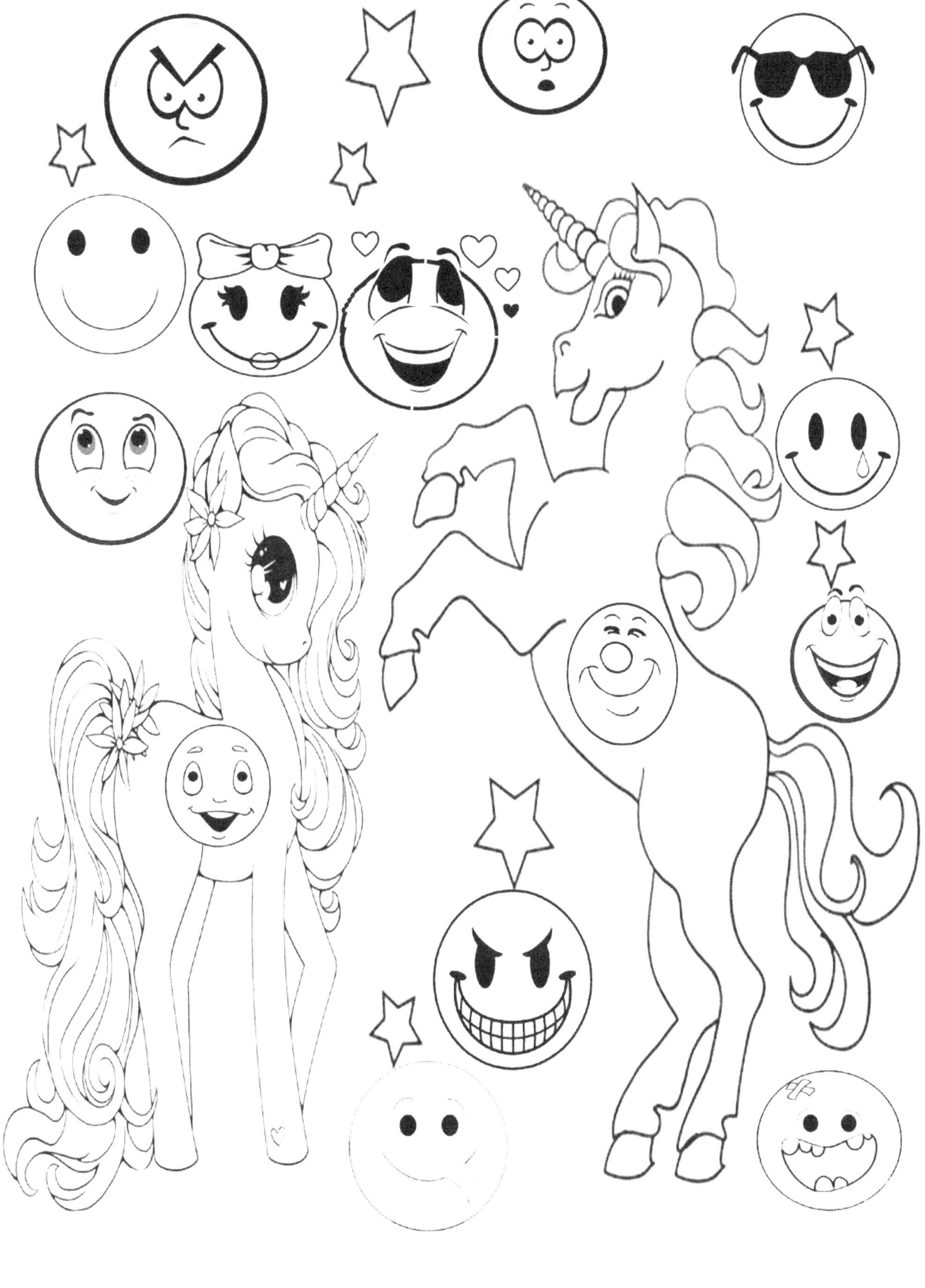

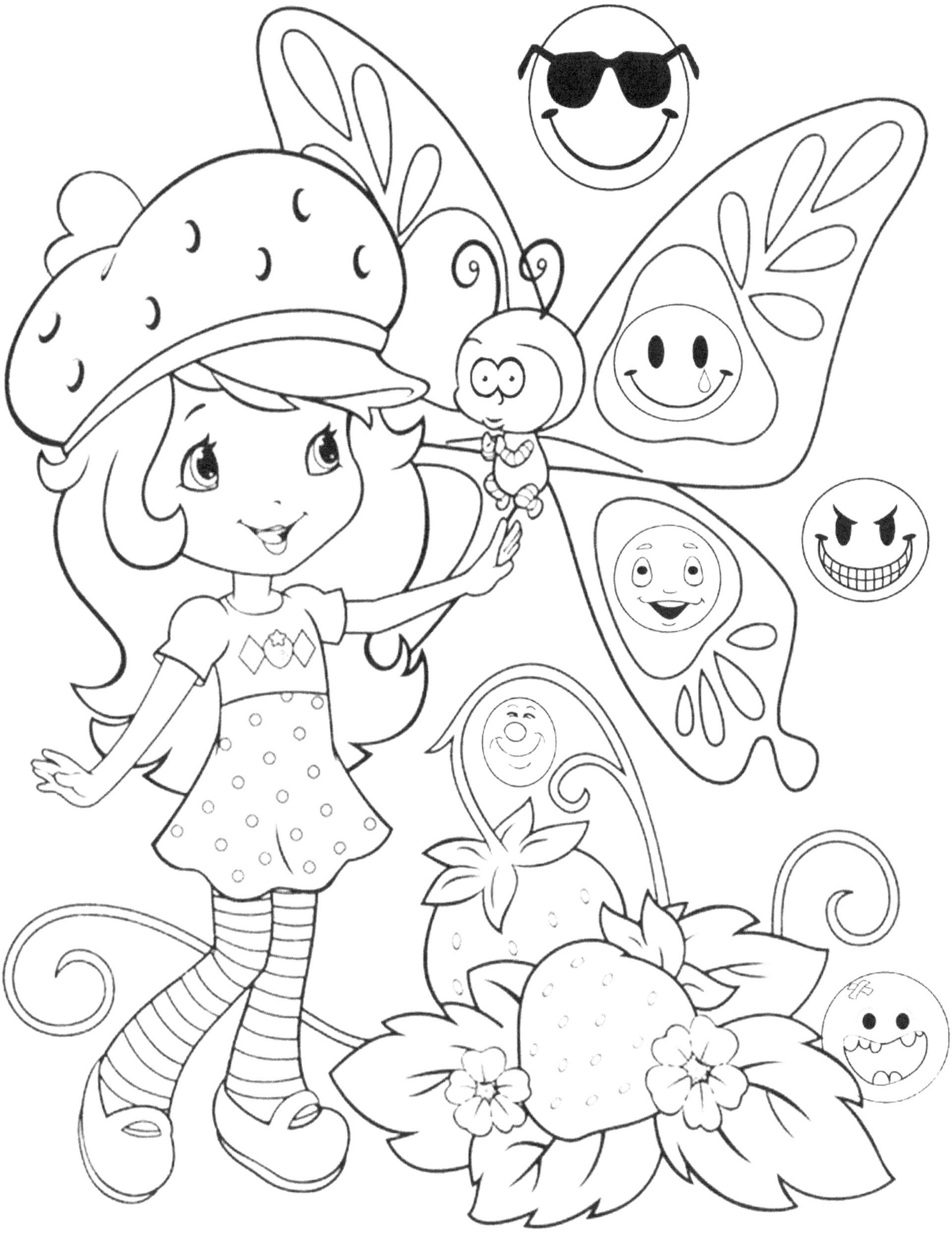

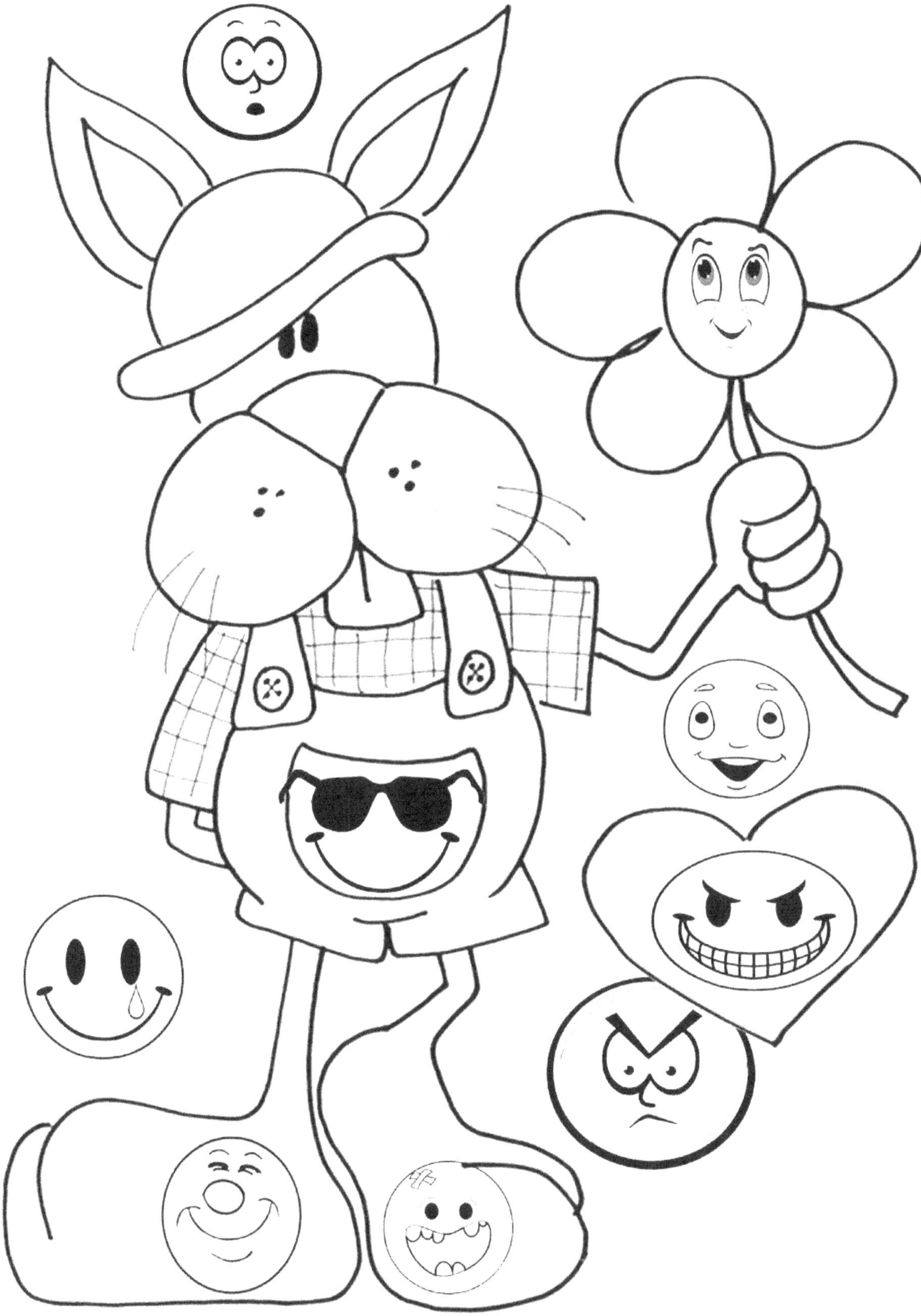

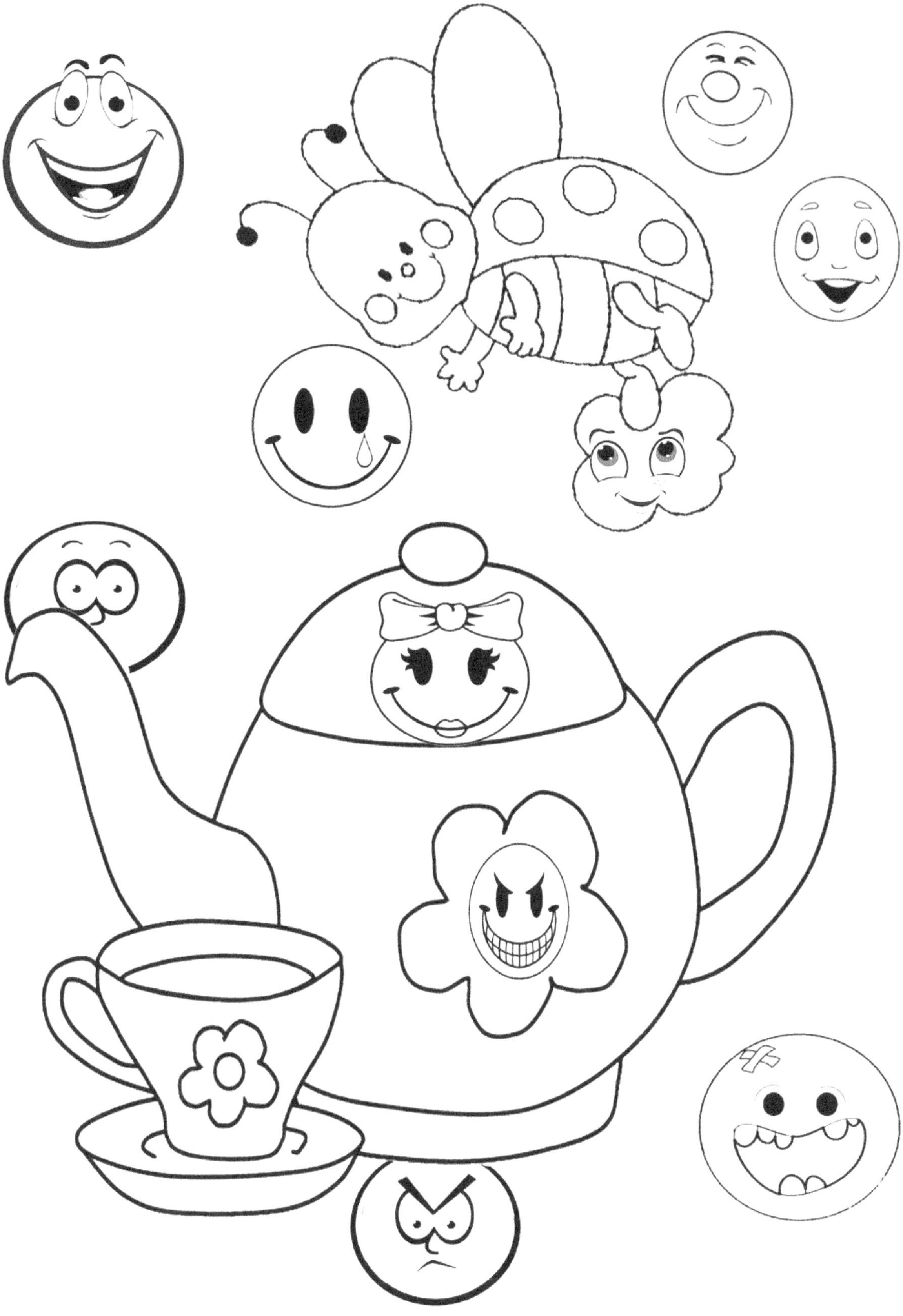

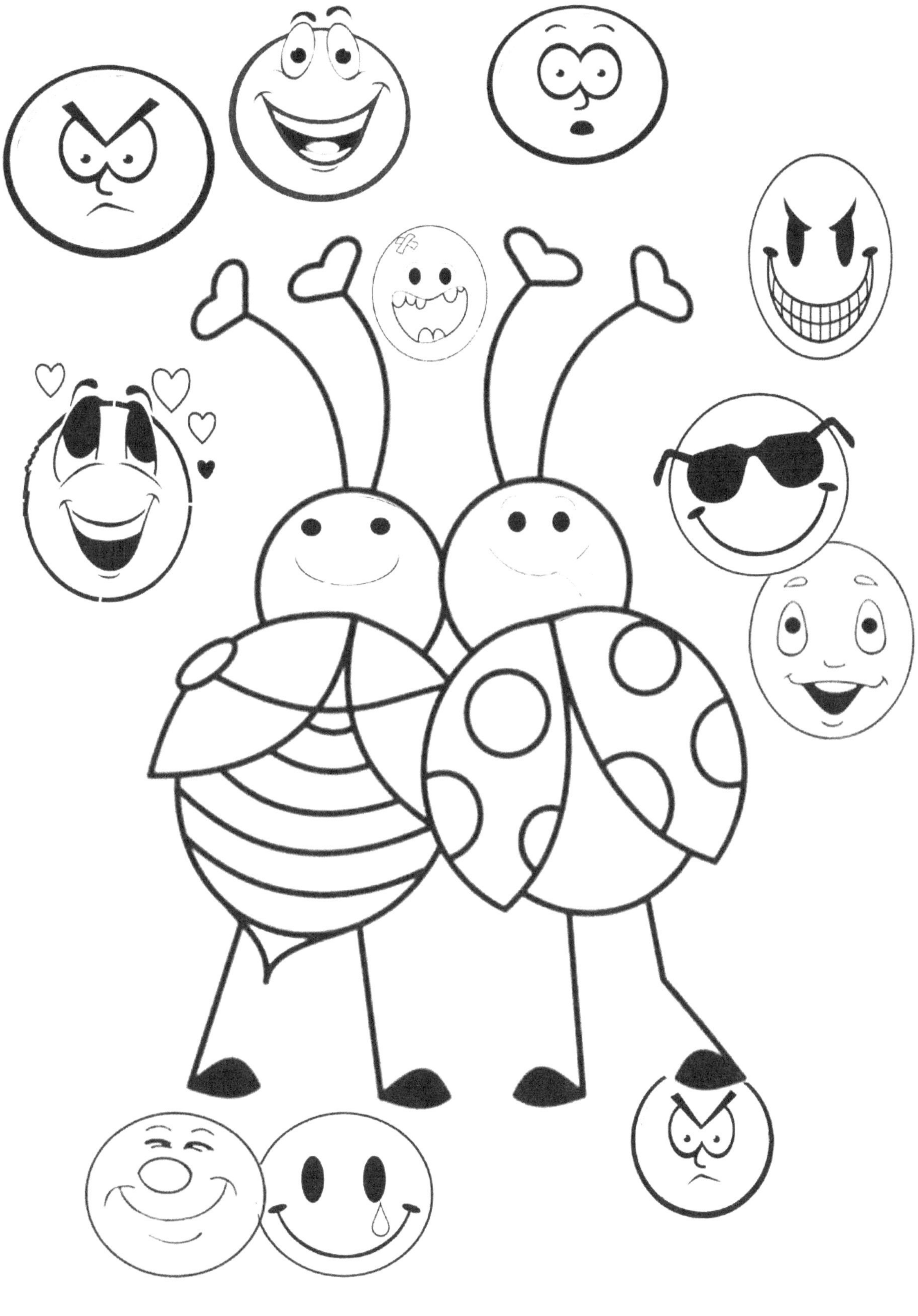

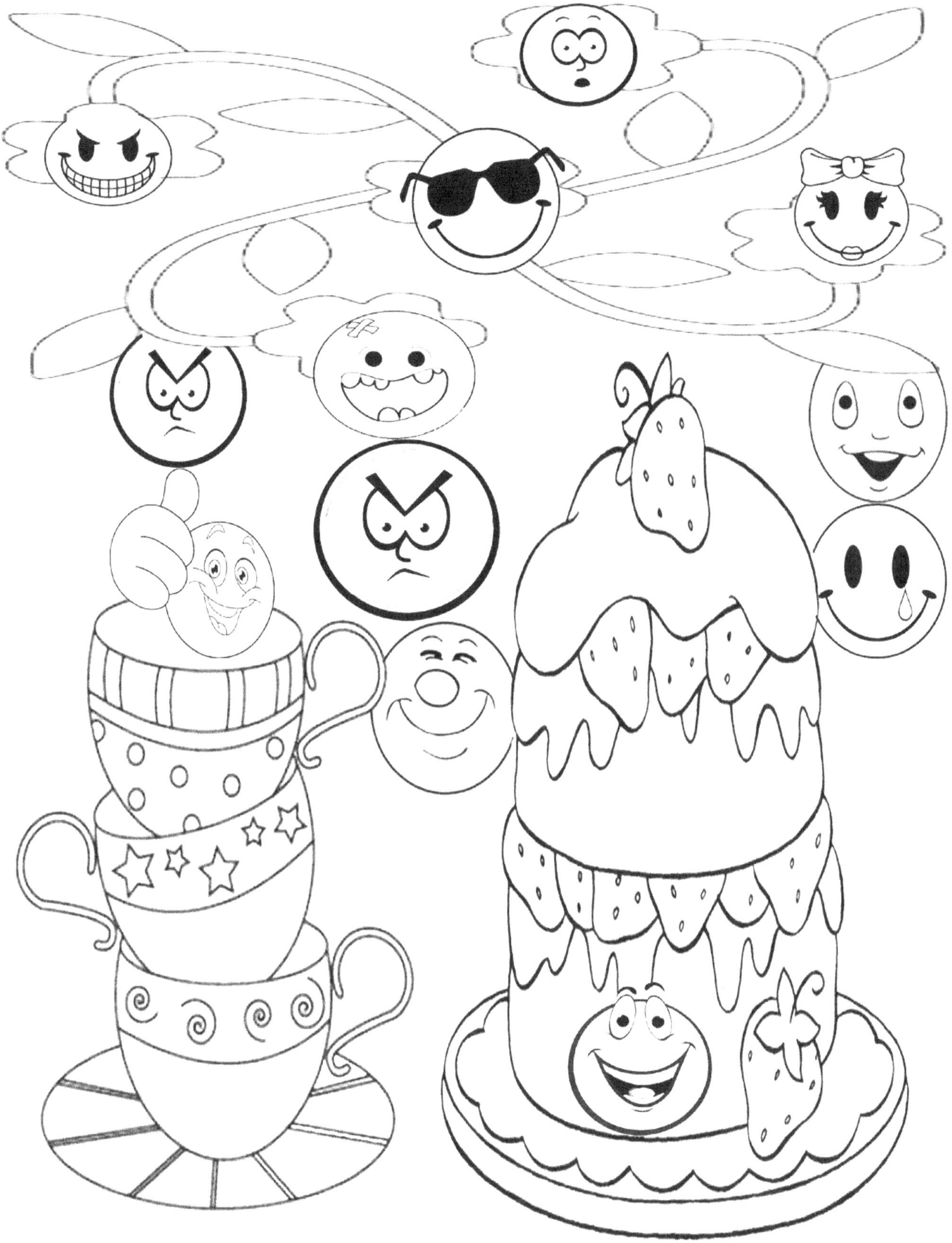

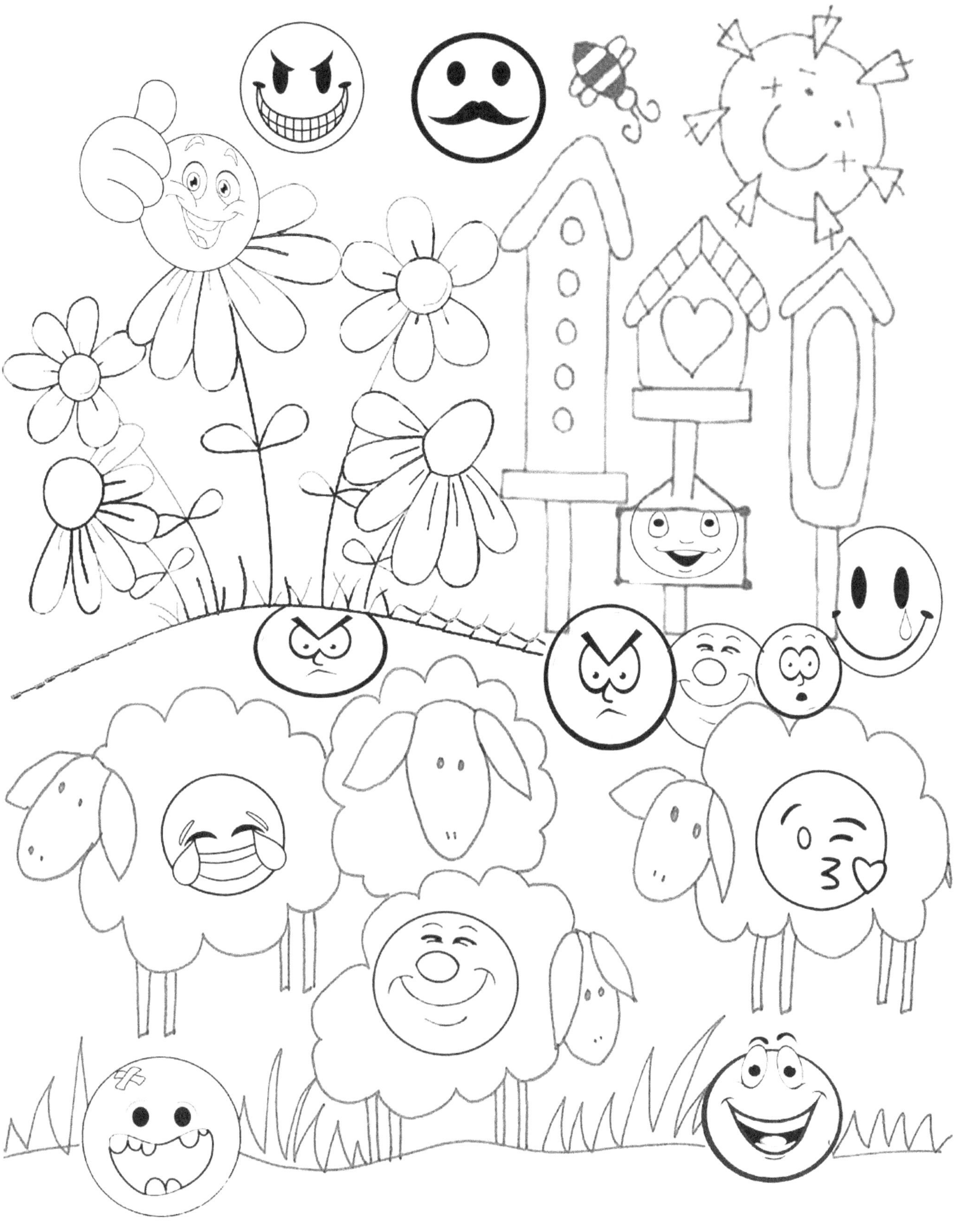

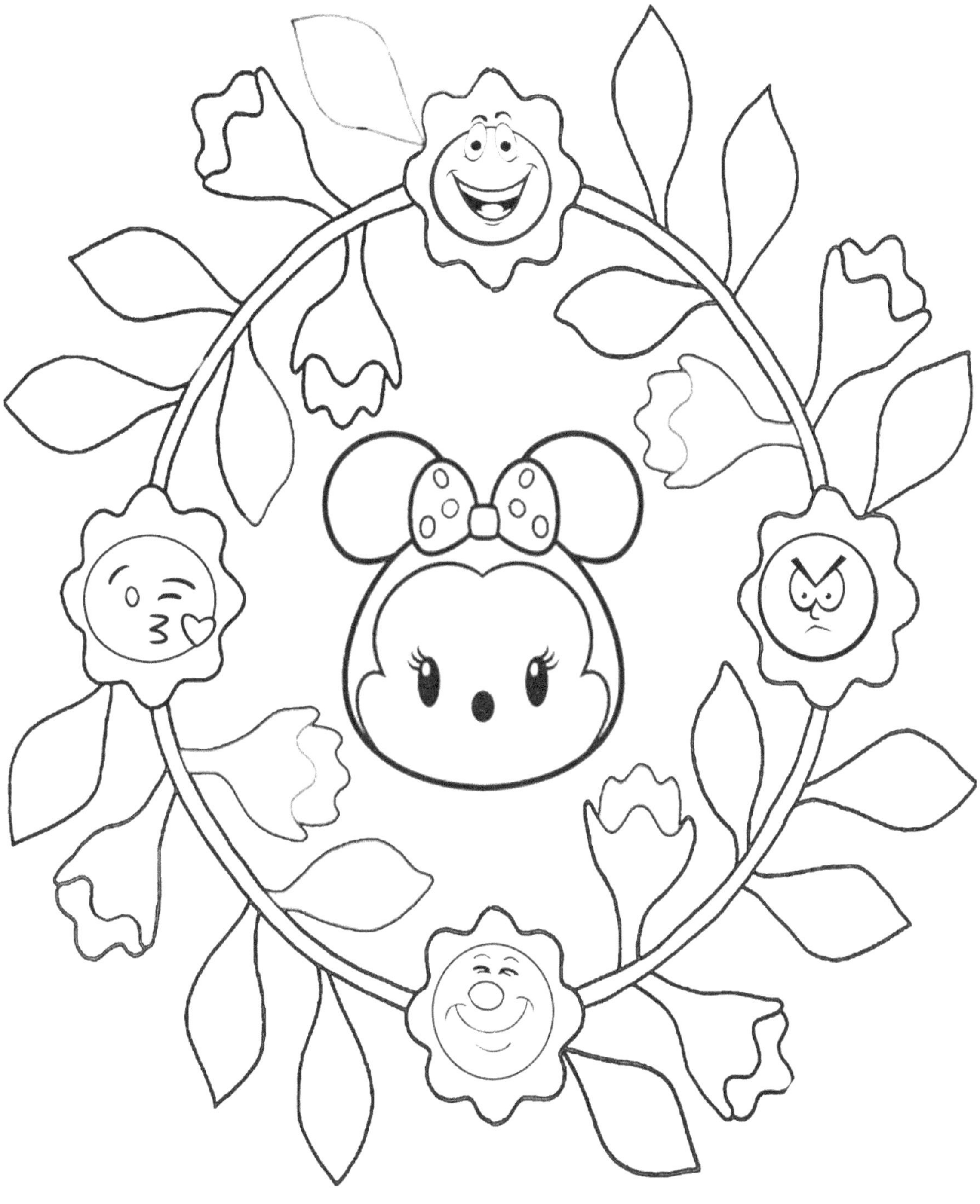

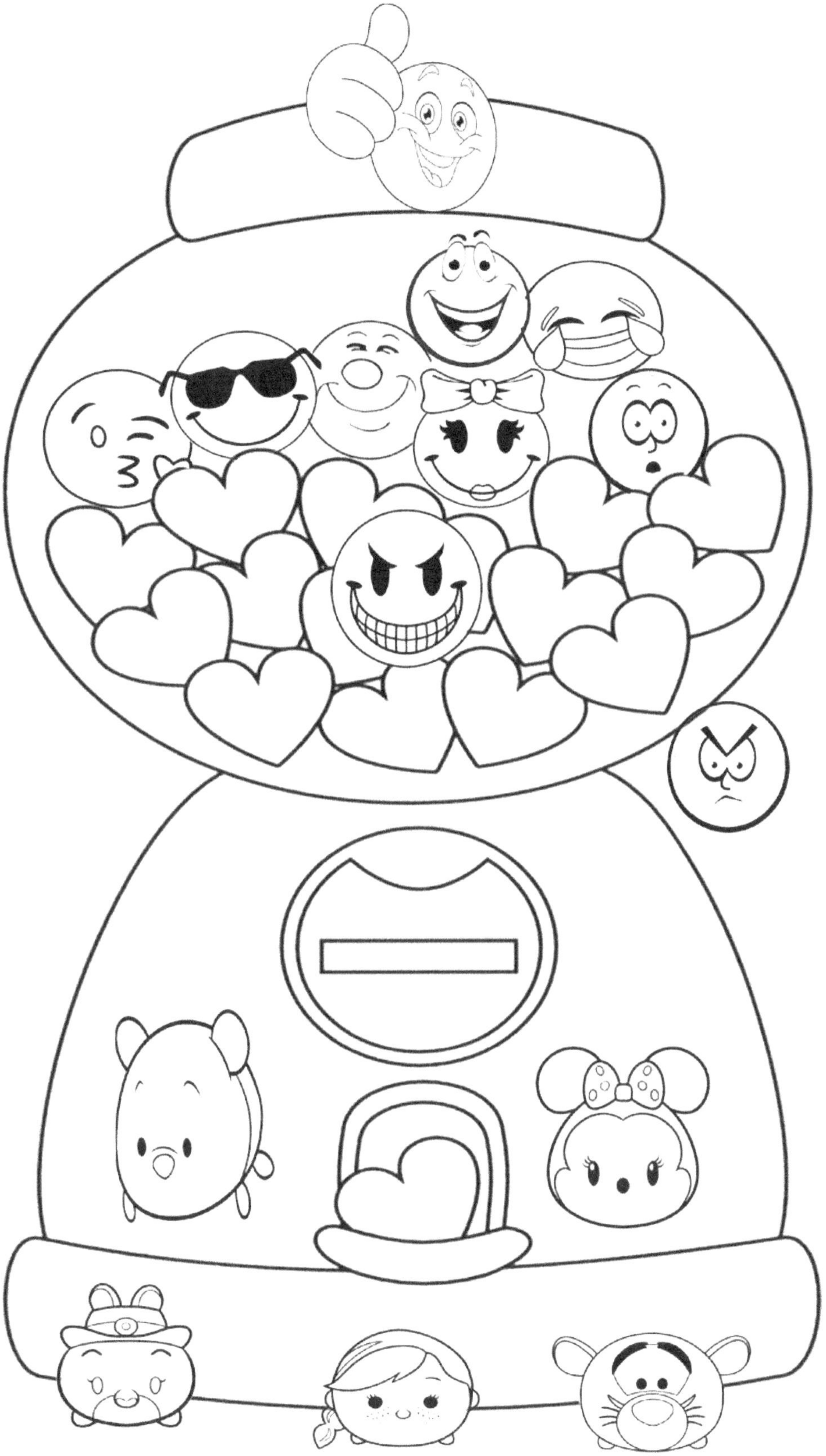

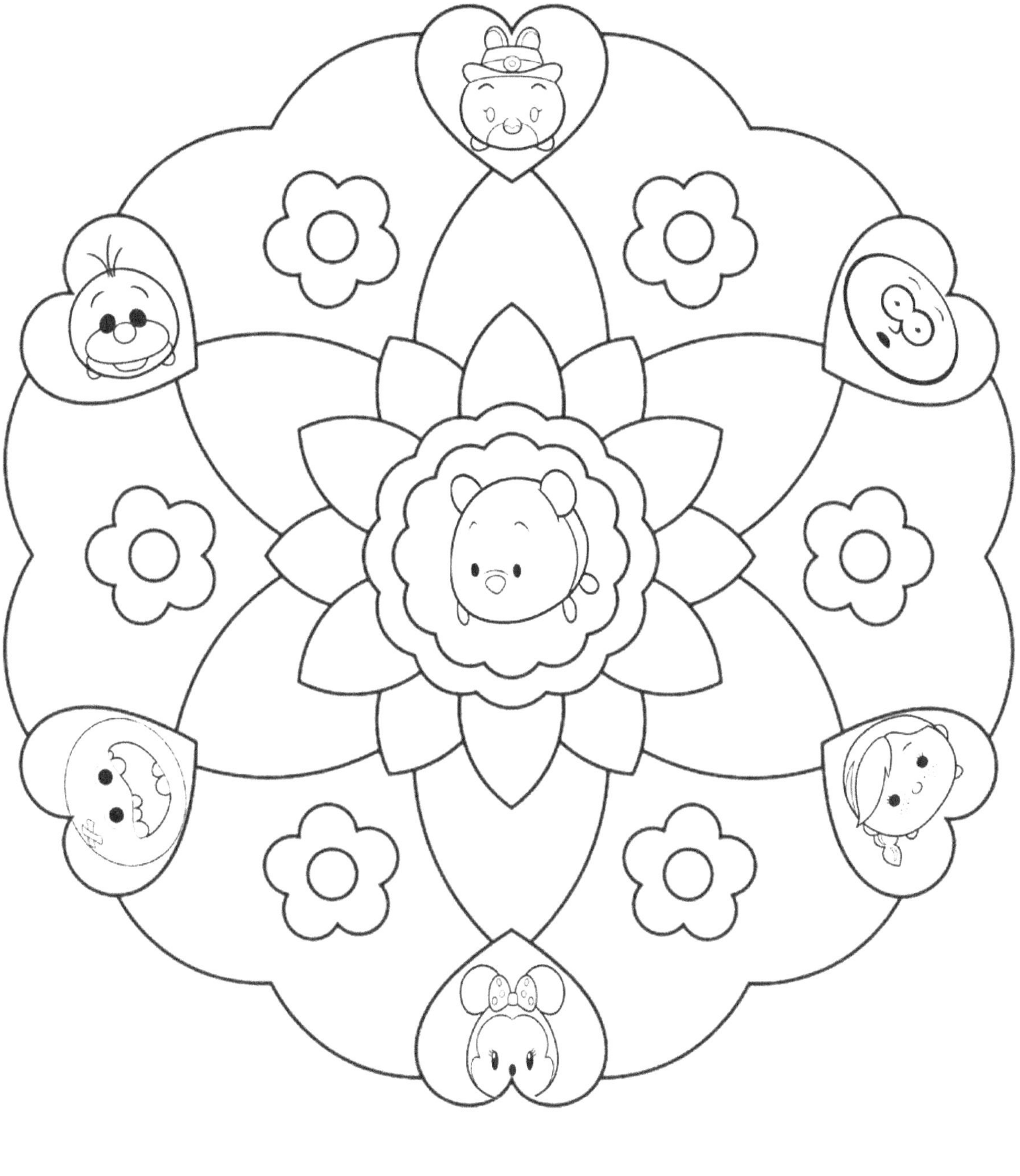

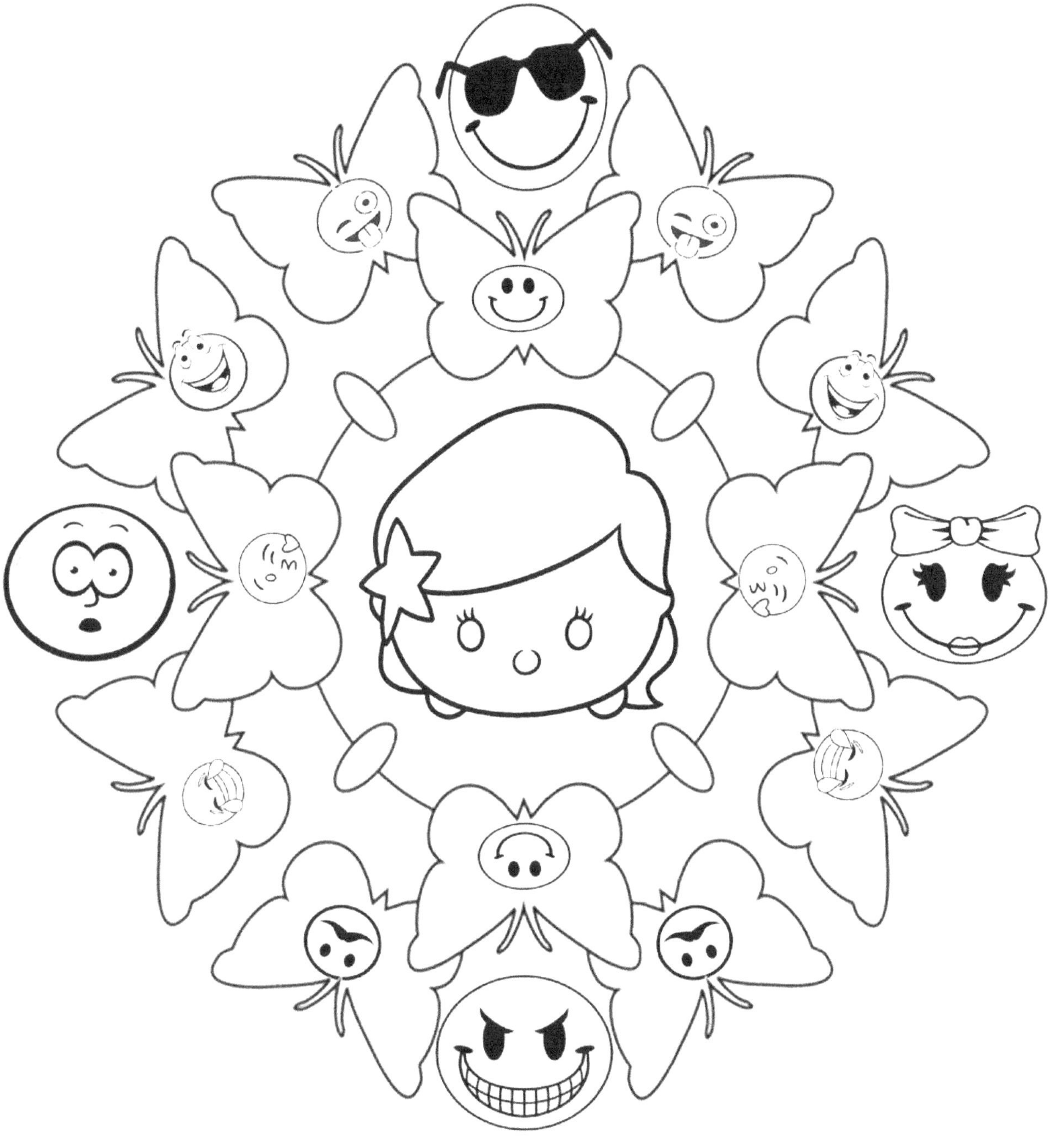

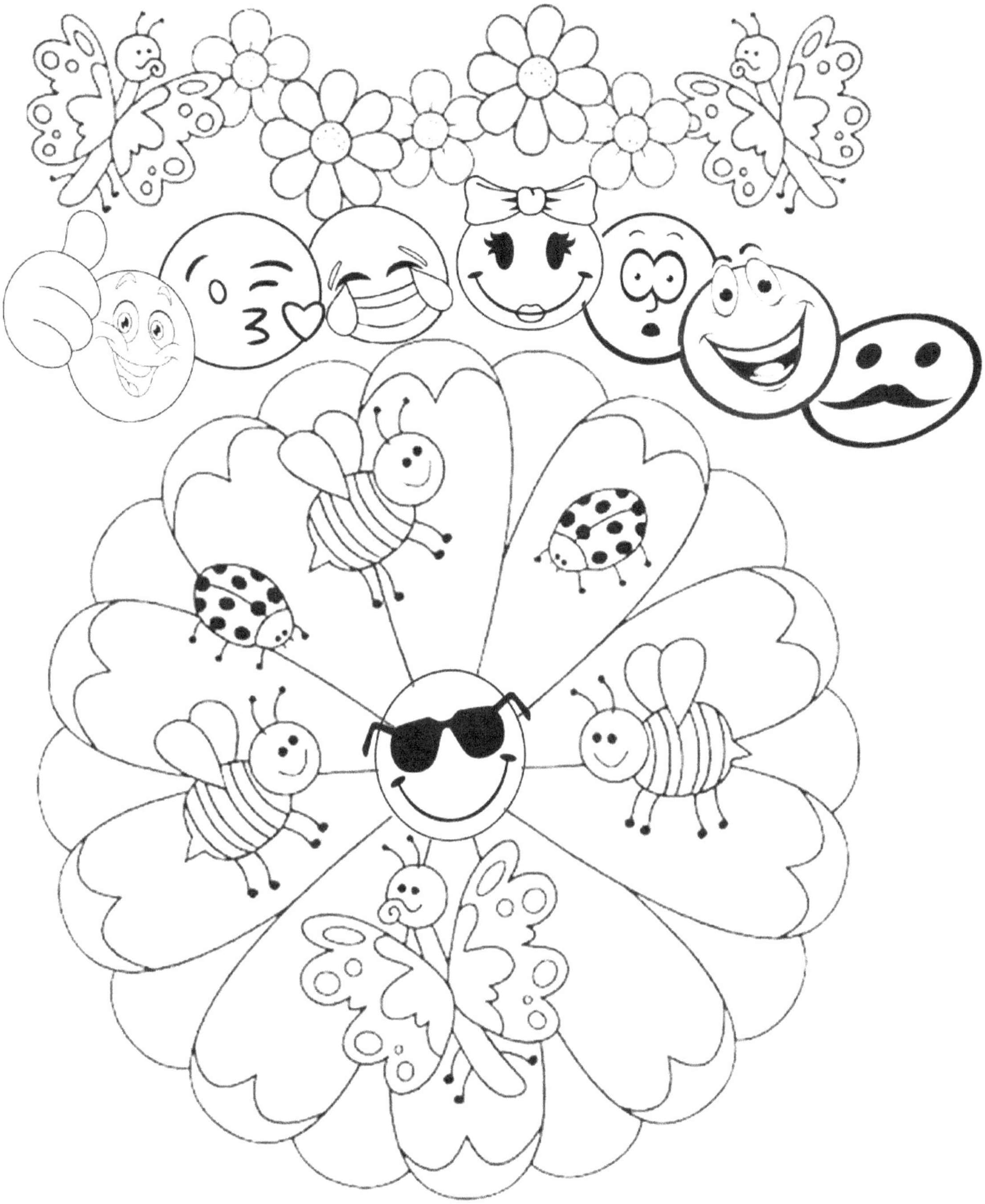

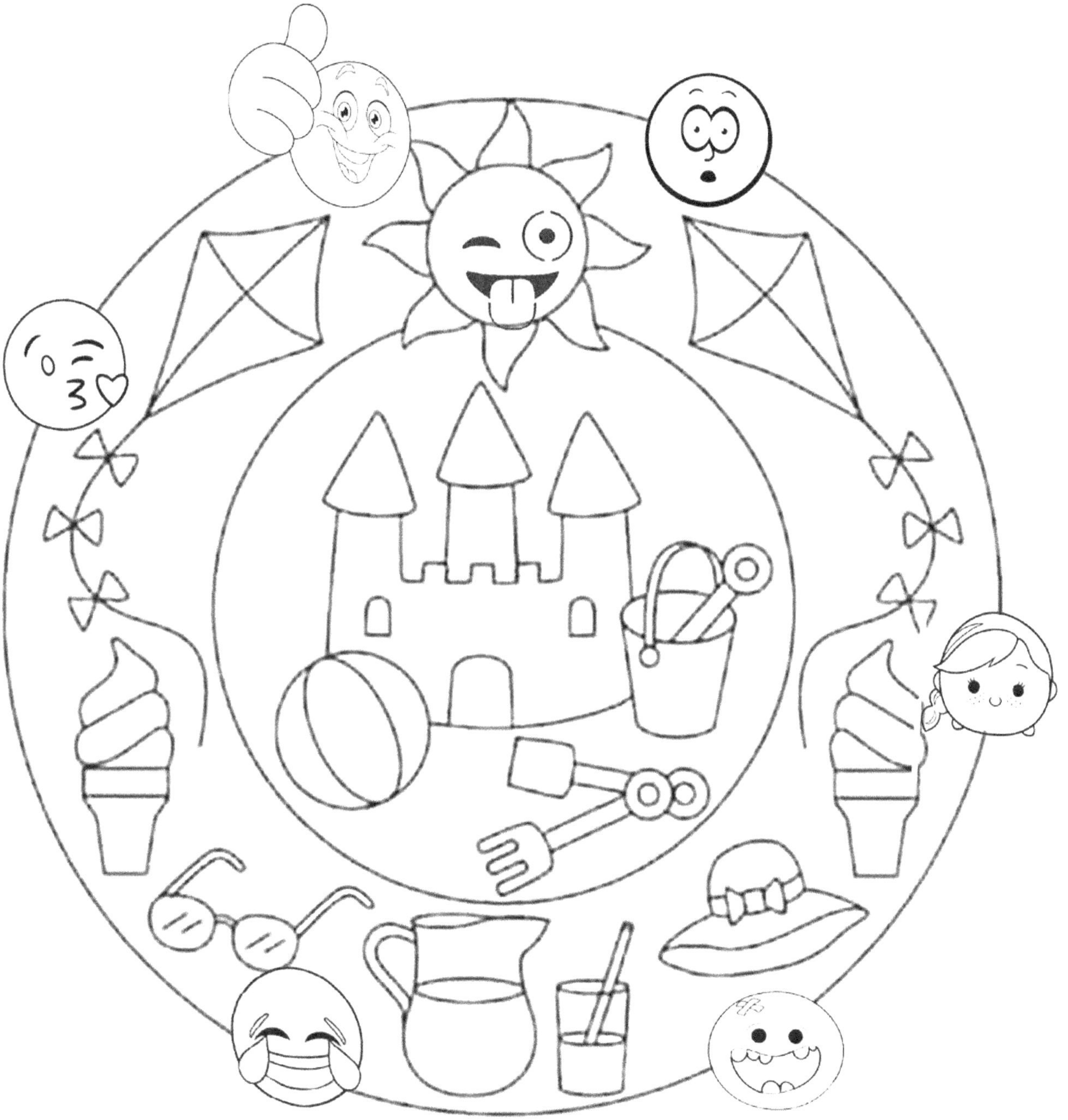

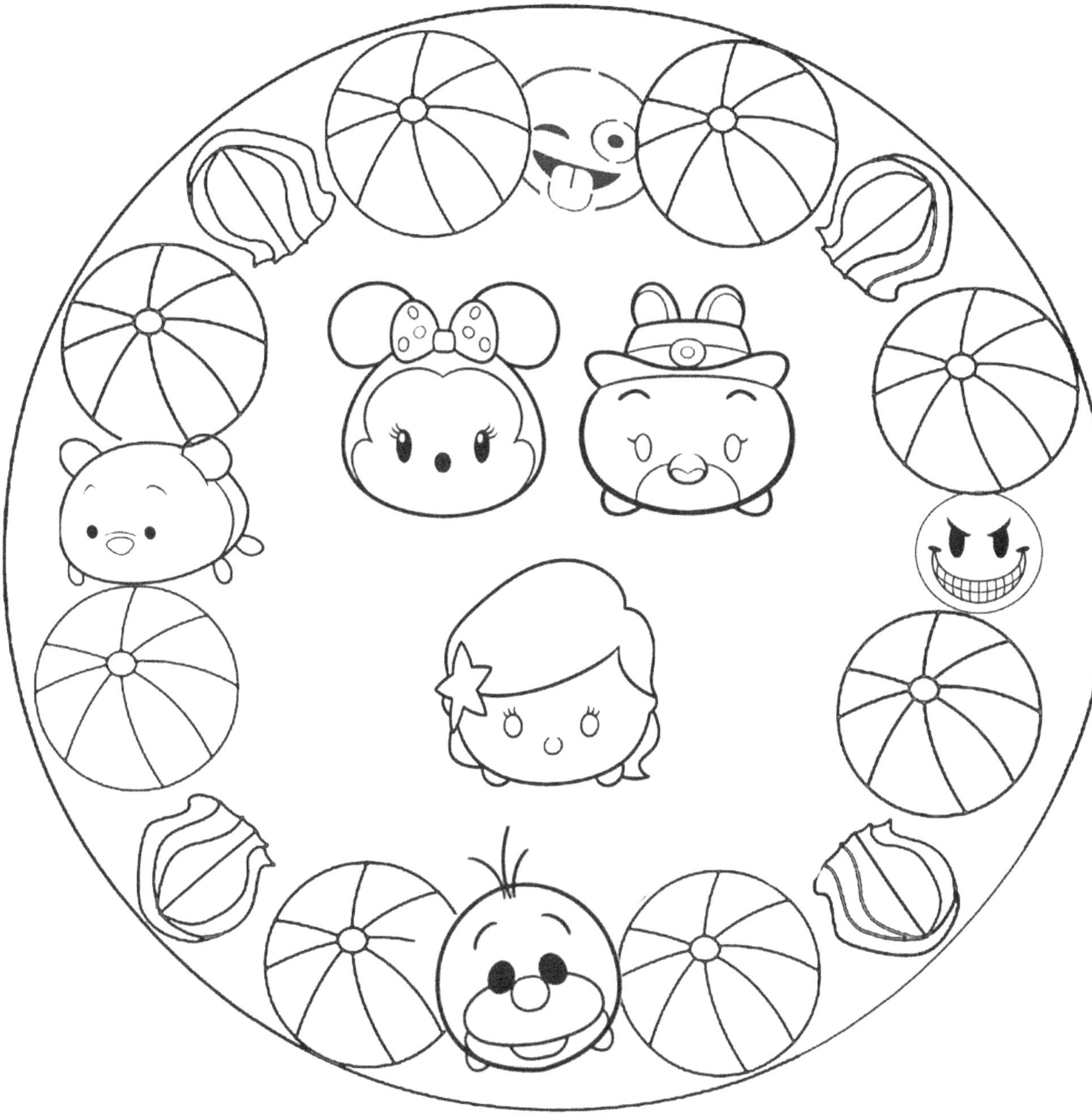

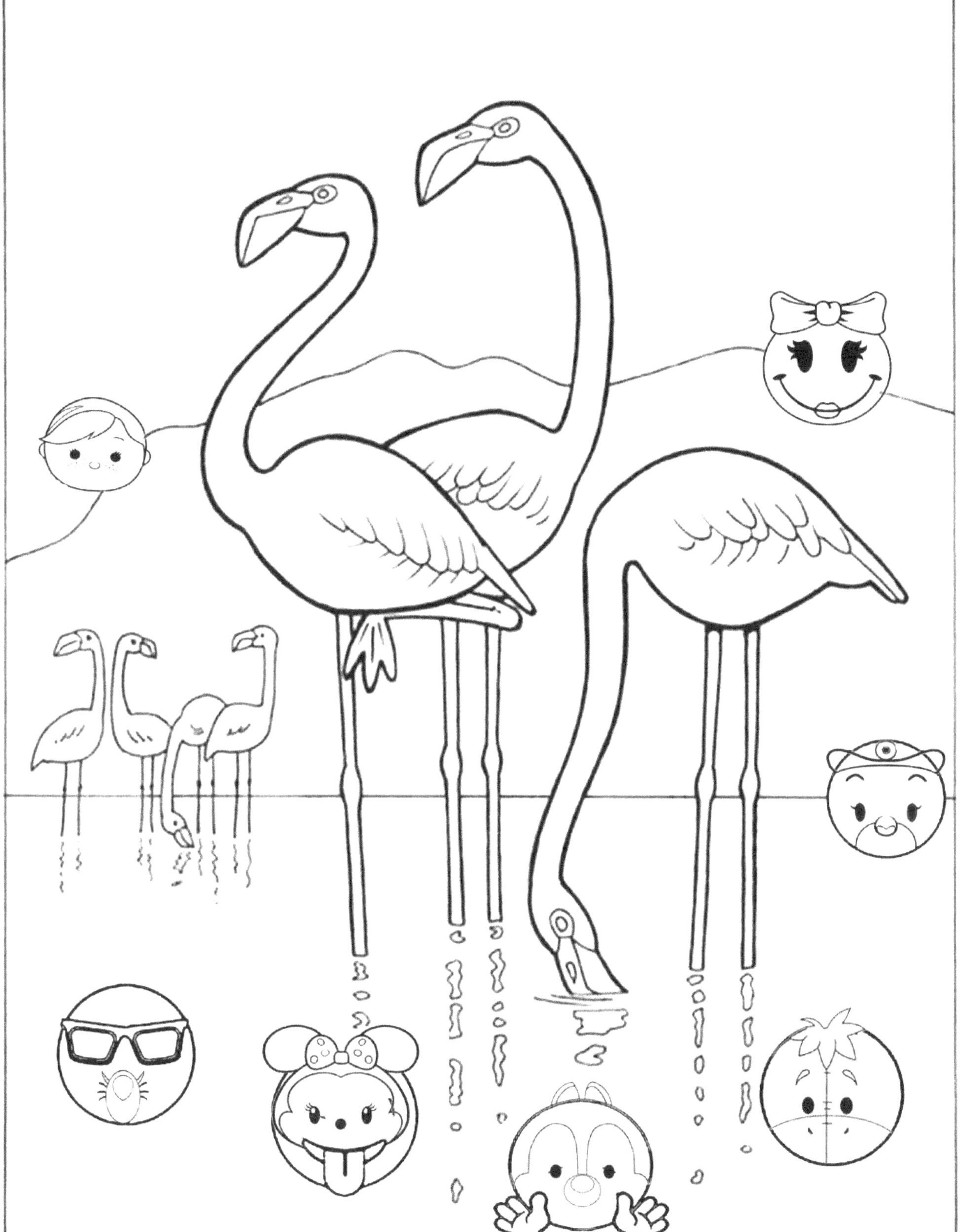

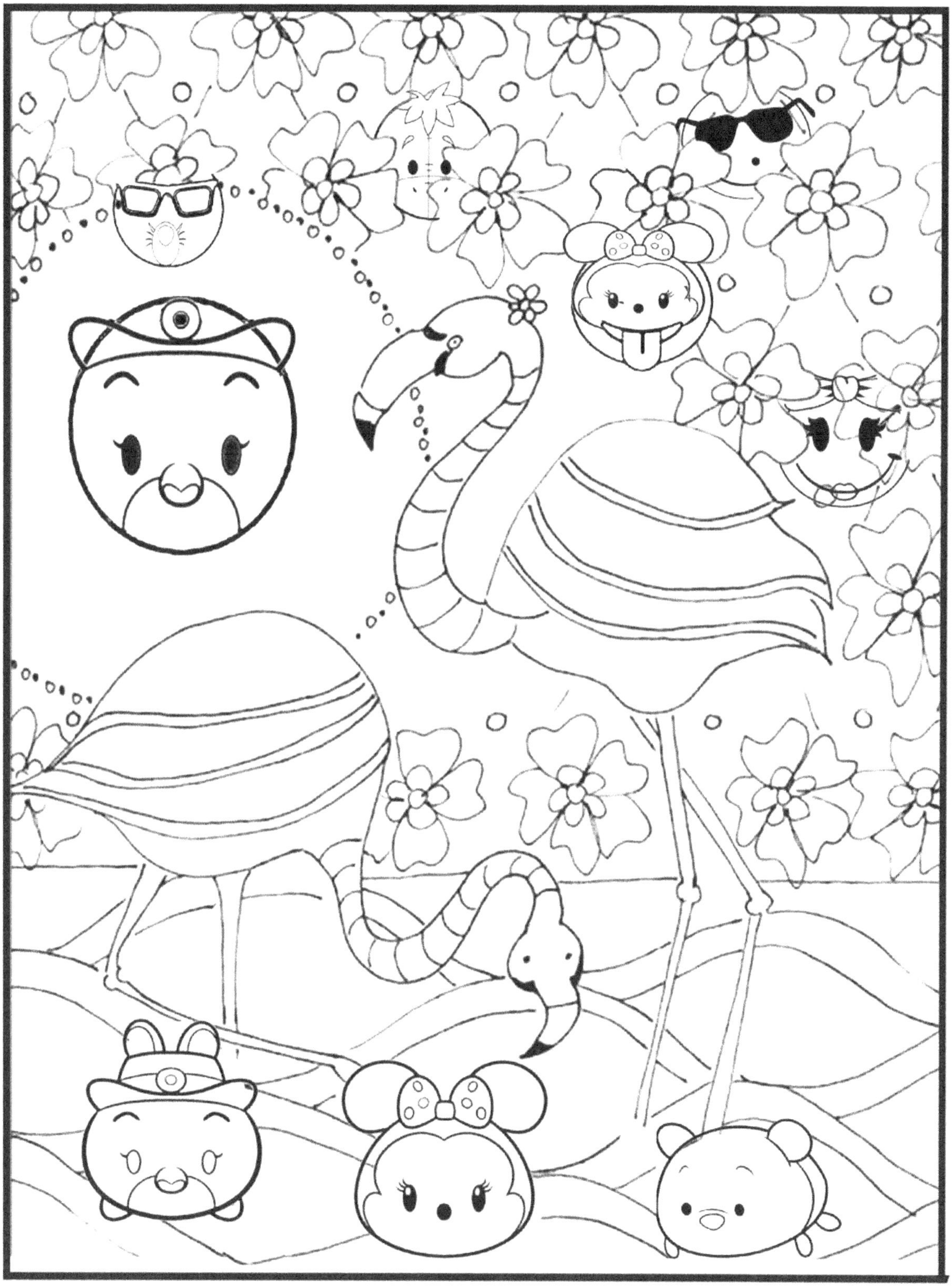

EMOJIS

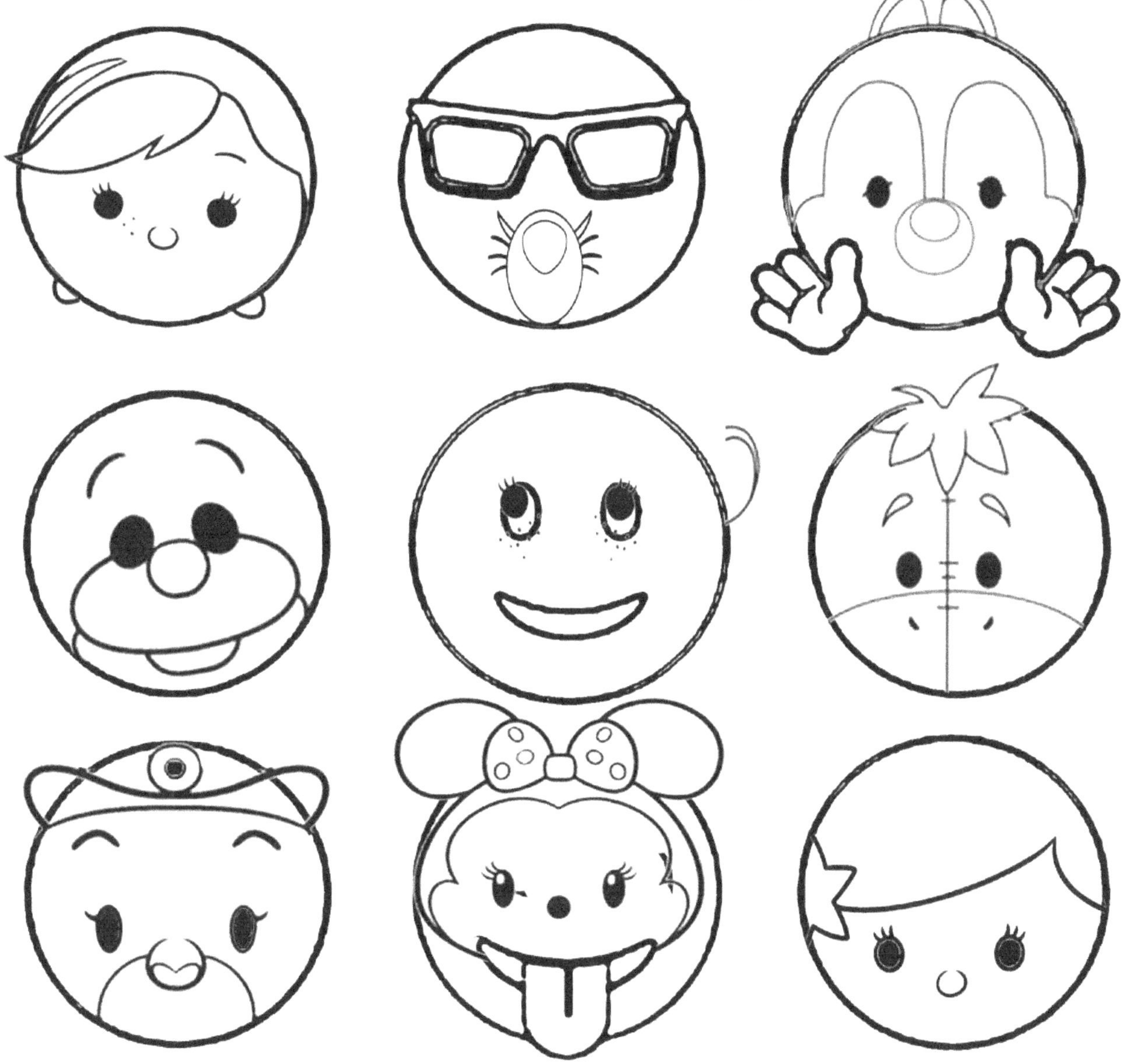

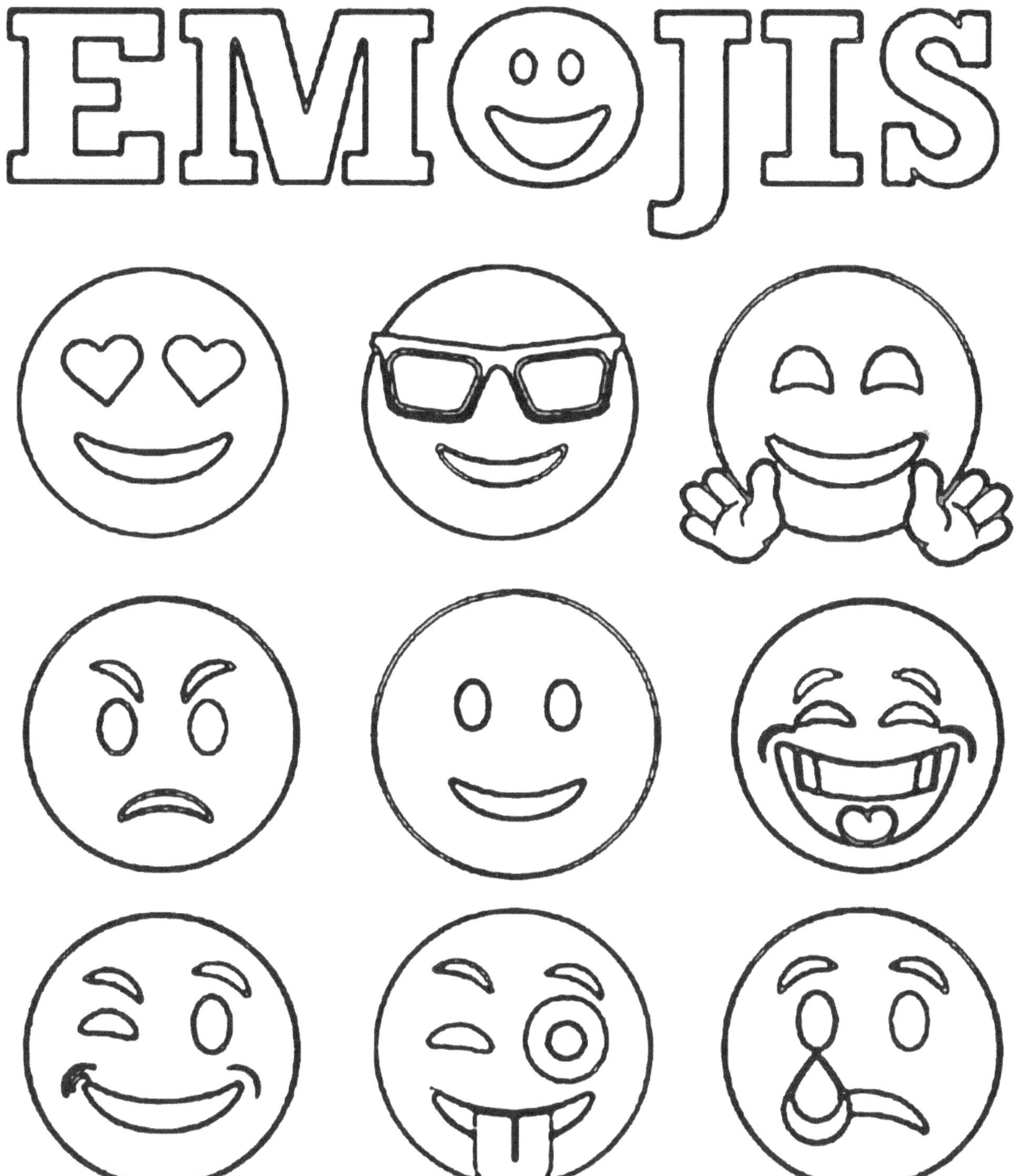
EMOJIS

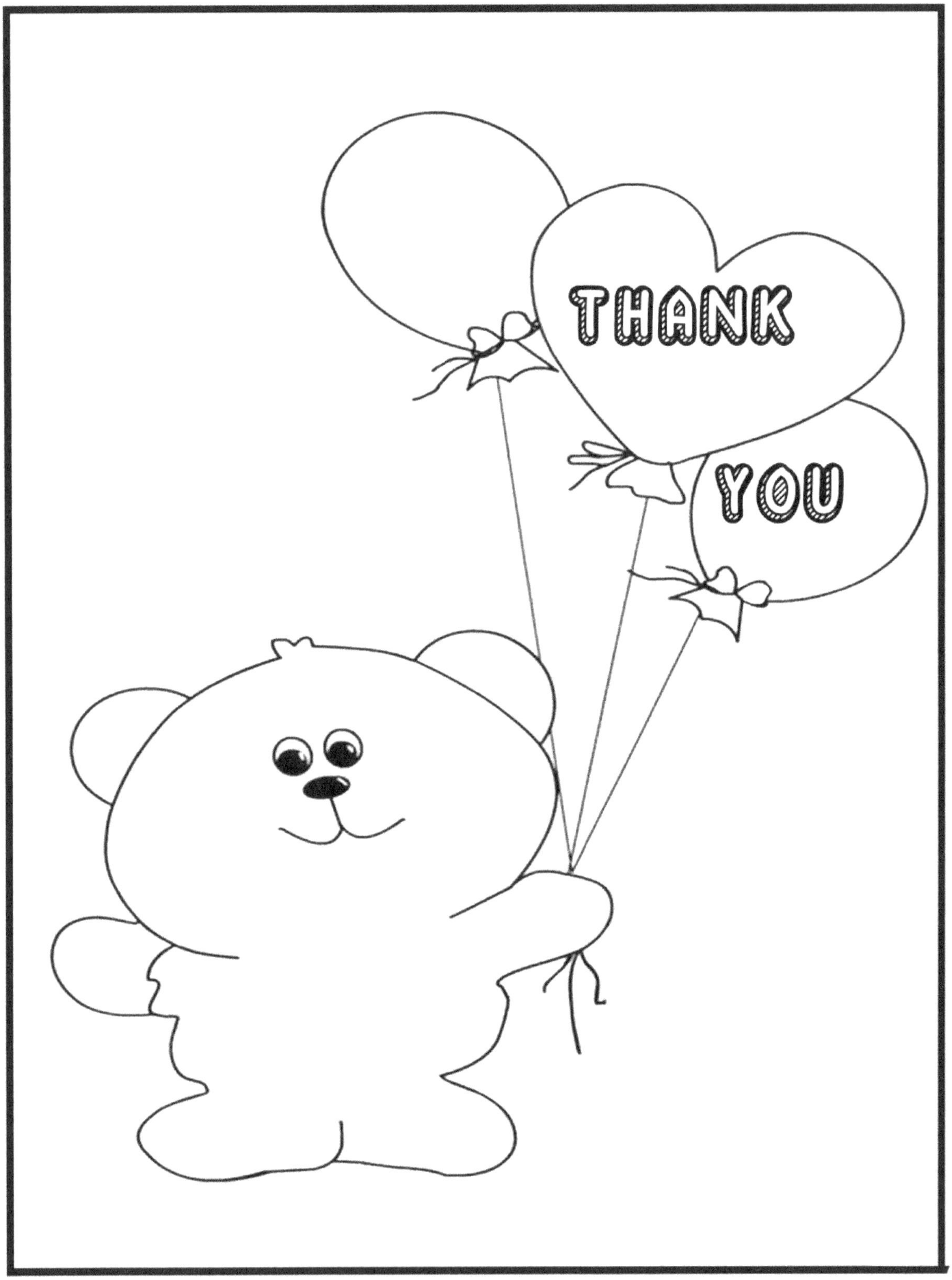
THANK
YOU

www.ingramcontent.com/pod-product-compliance
Lightning Source LLC
Chambersburg PA
CBHW081616220526
45468CB00010B/2906